The Frugal Gourmet
Keeps the Feast

T H E

Frugal Gourmet
Keeps the Feast
Past, Present, and Future

———•———

Recipes and Stories That Explain How the Ancient
Table May Be Celebrated in Our Time and How
Food Functions as Theological Talk in the Bible

Jeff Smith

Craig Wollam
Culinary Consultant

Chris Cart
Illustrator

William Morrow and Company, Inc.
New York

Library of Congress Cataloging-in-Publication Data

Smith, Jeff.
    The Frugal Gourmet keeps the feast : past, present, and future / by Jeff Smith.
        p.   cm.
    Includes index.
    ISBN 0-688-11568-3
    1. Cookery.   2. Food in the Bible.   I. Title.
    TX652.S5535 1995
    641.5—dc20   95-11075
                                                                                      CIP

Printed in the United States of America

First Edition

1 2 3 4 5 6 7 8 9 10

BOOK DESIGN BY RICHARD ORIOLO

This effort is dedicated to that very first class of students who joined me in a course I taught when university chaplain at the University of Puget Sound, Tacoma, Washington, in 1971. It was entitled "Food as Sacrament and Celebration."

Ida Ballasiotes

Reg Briggs

Nadine Callow

Chuck Churchward

Martha Coe

Becky Copeland

Marcia David

Bob Folker

Jon Hersh

Edie Hubbard

Diane Inman

Dave Kinman

Vickie Lundvall

Laurie McGee

Alison Scott

Jim Ulrich

Tom Wiberg

I shall never forget that bunch! Thank you.

Acknowledgments

It is hard to talk of the Feast when so many that I wish to call to the table have died. But the Feast can continue through the memory of their presence and what they have taught me.

The faculty at the Drew University School of Theology during the 1960s was the best Biblical faculty in the country at the time. They brought me to my theological senses. I thank them, especially:

John Drew Godsey, Systematic Theology

Howard Clark Kee, New Testament

Robert Bull, Church History

John Paterson, Old Testament

Lawrence E. Toombs, Old Testament

Franz Hildebrandt, Wesleyan Theology

James Ranck, Pastoral Psychology

Al Haas, Worship and Liturgics

Gordon Harland, Church History

Nelle Morton, Christian Education

Carl Michelson, Hermeneutical Theology

David James Randolf, Homiletics

Bernard Word Anderson, Old Testament

Robert Carrigan, Pastoral Psychology

Charles Wesley Ranson, Ecumenics

Will Herberg, Sociology of Religion

Only seven of the above scholars are still alive, but this whole community speaks to me almost every day. I am thankful.

I have already mentioned my appreciation for that first class of students in Food and Theology at the University of Puget Sound, Tacoma, Washington. I have dedicated this book to them.

Further, several other colleagues at UPS were terribly helpful to me through the years as I contemplated this subject. John Magee, Esther Wagner, Bob Albertson, and John Philips were each a blessing.

R. F. Capon (see Bibliography) got me going on this project and Lester Baskin fed me through the years with wine and food and affection. And Sara Little Turnbull, a dear friend, has always been ready with the line, "Jeffrey, let's talk about what you have just said!"

Ann Bramson, my editor at William Morrow, has been very helpful and more than patient, as has our head man and good friend, Al Marchioni. Bill Adler, who has been my book agent through all of these years, continues to nod "yes" whenever I tell him of a new idea.

I thank Christ Church Parish, Tacoma, and St. Mark's Cathedral, Seattle, for listening to these ideas through the years, and thanks as well to the dozens of groups, particularly in the United Methodist Church, who have asked me to speak about this subject.

Blessings and thanks to Craig Wollam, my associate of eight years and eight cookbooks. His remark on this one? "You've sure got a lot of cracked wheat and yogurt in this one, Doctor!" Thanks, Craig.

My regular office staff is almost another family for me. Polly Withers, our administrative assistant—from London yet—helped edit. James Paddleford, our business manager, is a very decent theologian in his own right and he was insightful at every point. Finally, our kitchen man, a graduate of the Culinary Institute of America, Tim Peterson, is also a religion major from St. Olaf College. He smirks a lot at what I have written but he is helpful in the kitchen and at the editing desk.

Most important, I must thank my family, especially Patty, my wife, for her constant insights. The four of us spend more time together at table than at any other place. We have celebrated Seder, Yom Kippur, Christmas, Greek Easter, and a hundred holy festivals based on other cultures. Through all of this, the boys have never thought me to be weird; at least they have never expressed such a thought out loud. Thank you, fellows!

"LORD, KEEP US ALIVE AS LONG AS WE LIVE!"

Contents

Introduction

I started to think about the theme of this book at least thirty years ago. I thought about it during my years in graduate school in theology and during the years that I taught theology at a university. I have thought about it during the twenty years that I have been doing television cooking shows, and I think about it each time I prepare a feast for family and friends.

I am often asked why I left the ministry and started a television cooking show. I have *not* left the ministry. I just don't have a local parish. My orders are in order with the United Methodist Church, and I preach and teach regularly. Further, I always try to offer some theological insights when I teach cooking on television. I always have.

This is how the transition from college chaplain to television cooking instructor took place: While I was a college chaplain during the late sixties, I realized that my students were eating poorly because they were sinking all of their money into the peace movement. Since I had always been fond of the kitchen, I began serving Sunday feasts after University Church. The students packed our home each weekend, and I began to teach them how to cook in a frugal manner. Now, remember, frugal does not mean cheap, it means that you don't waste anything.

During the time of these feasts, I was assigned a course in the religion department, a course on worship. We began to discuss the fact that little has been written in American theology about the history of the Biblical table. Why? One of our students came up with the answer in the form of a book review of R. F. Capon's *The Supper of the Lamb.* You must read this totally celebrative book that so enjoys the table (see Bibliography). Capon got me started.

The next semester we designed a class called Food as Sacrament and Celebration. It filled each semester before the catalog was printed.

You see, I have always been much more interested in theology than in food.

When I was in graduate school in theology I began to think about the way the Bible uses food to discuss theology. This book and the whole concept of the Frugal Gourmet are the result of those days at Drew University School of Theology. Lord knows I have taken a lot of time to jot down these insights.

The other day an American Airlines Special Services rep was escorting us through Kennedy Airport. "What's the next book you are doing, Frug?" "It's called *The Frugal Gourmet Keeps the Feast.* Does that title interest you?" "Well, sure," this lovely Italian woman replied. "And I assume you are going to cook pasta in Holy Water." Well, not quite.

The path from chaplain to television cook has been a very sensible trip for me. I hope that the articles that follow make it plain that I love theology and feasting with friends. The two belong together, and the table is the best center for celebrating our place as children of God.

I bid you peace,
Jeff Smith

The Table as Communication

Food Talk as God Talk

The Bible is filled with Food Talk, but the Bible is not talking about food. It is talking about theology, or God Talk.

The word *faith* is used about 275 times in the Bible . . . but the verb *to eat* is used some 800 times.

Jesus never says, "Behold, I stand at the door and knock. If anyone should open the door, I will enter and discuss existential theology with him." No. Jesus says, "I will sup with him."

All of the Resurrection appearances occurred at table, with that one exception of the appearance at the tomb. The rest were at meals: on the road to Emmaus, in the Upper Room, the fish fry on the edge of the Sea of Galilee.

Food Talk in the Old Testament

Why all of this food talk in the Bible? Actually, the Bible is not talking about food when it talks about food. Rather, it is talking theology.

The word *theology* simply means "God Talk." *Theos* refers to God, and *logos*, or *ology*, means "words about." It seems like such a strange form of communication, but actually it is quite profound and practical. I will offer several reasons why Food Talk is actually God Talk in the Bible.

The first reason is due to the nature of the Hebrew language. It is a very concrete language, a language that grew out of life on the desert, and it has few, if any, universals. That is to say, if you could not point to it in the physical sense, then you could not speak about it . . . unless you symbolized or mythologized that thing to which you were trying to point.

Here's an example that certainly shows how useful food images are in communication in the Bible.

In the ancient world salt was used as a preservative, and therefore it became a symbol of friendship.

Here is the picture: You have a neighbor whom you really dislike but you know that you must learn to deal with this person, even appreciate him. But you have a conflict: You raise roses and he has a bulldog. It is not a pretty thought.

Finally, you invite this person over for a glass of sherry and you begin the explanation. You can say this in English, German, French, Latin, Spanish, whatever, but you cannot talk this way in Hebrew. "I am so glad that you could come over for a sherry. I too have become ambiguously anxious over the state of alienation and separation that has come between us due to the proximity of our mutual concerns and our inability to understand one another's position." You cannot even *say* that in Hebrew because the statement is filled with universals and generalities. You have to be concrete. In order to accomplish the same thing, if you were living in old Jerusalem, you would have invited your neighbor over and extended a dish of salt. Each of you would lick your finger and dip it in the salt and then eat the salt together. There! This symbol of friendship healed the rift. Heavy and confusing talk was not necessary, not then.

You understand what I mean, I am sure. And you also understand the problem with language. There are certain things in our lives that are very real—they are true experiences—yet they do not exist in the same way as the chair in the front room exists. They are hard to point to and so we come up with phrases like "You know what I mean."

The Bible is filled with such problems with language to express the indescribable. It offers some wonderful solutions in the form of symbols and stories when communicating about those things that really matter but are not physical in the usual sense.

The Old Testament is rich with paradoxical language, particularly oxymorons. These put two contradictory words together in order to say something that neither term could say on its own, such as good grief or painful joy. Consider the fun that can be had with oxymorons. We all know what these words mean, and there seem to be few other ways to clearly express our feelings about a particular situation or experience. The Bible is fond of the term *easy yoke,* which refers to the yoke that cattle must wear when pulling heavy burdens. But the writer tells us that the burden of being a Child of the Kingdom is an "easy yoke." He is implying some kind of magnificent help here.

You use oxymorons all the time, and some of them are funny. Painful joy I understand, such as trying to be patient with your two sons. But joyful pain sounds a bit kinky to me. You know what I mean. The Frugal Gourmet is one of my favorite oxymorons.

The Old Testament's favorite oxymoron seems to be the name of God. Now, remember that you cannot point to God since God is beyond that which we call existence. Existence means that you are now, but there will be a time when you will not exist. The term God refers to that One that is before existence and beyond. So I suppose you can say that God does not exist as you and I do, but God certainly is!

Since one cannot point to God, and since the Hebrew language is so very concrete, how does one speak of God? The oxymoron that the Old Testament uses is just a gem. God is referred to as "The Holy One of Israel," a term that probably doesn't shake you up very much. But it should. The term for "holy" in

Hebrew is *Qadosh (Kadosh)*. It refers to that which is totally beyond us, above and beyond all else that exists, so distant that it cannot be approached, in any way, shape, or form. "Of Israel" means here in town, made local for us by the Holy One's own choice, down on the corner!

Other languages, such as English, French, German, or Latin, can philosophize about the name of God and thus we come up with some odd titles and concepts. "God is the Ontological answer to the Existential question!" You can't even say that in Hebrew. What can you say? "The Lord is the rock upon which I stand." If the rock is removed I will fall forever. It means the same thing as the ontological answer to the existential question.

I had a wonderful teacher in Old Testament in graduate school. His name was Dr. John Patterson, and he was an old Scottish Presbyterian. He was so firm about the necessity of speaking clearly when in the pulpit that he once admonished us to never pray a prayer from the pulpit that could not be translated into Hebrew. He claimed that he once heard a young preacher address God as "Oh Great Working Hypothesis." The good Presbyterian then spat out his words and we all howled. You cannot talk of God like that in Hebrew. There are no words for such nonsense. Enough of this general theological type language! He had had it! Speak of God in the concrete, as do the Jews, and we can understand one another. I have never forgotten his advice.

There! I think I have made my point. You cannot talk of those things which are real but which do not exist in the normal physical form in Hebrew unless you symbolize.

Food as Language

So, at last we get into the food. Bear with me.

Food is one of the classic images we use to talk about fulfillment and loss, or hunger. When you claim that you are so hungry that you can eat a horse you certainly expect those around you to know that you are speaking of a very serious truth, though you are not being factual. So it is with food talk in the Bible.

All kinds of food products in the Bible become devices for pointing away from themselves to something else that one cannot speak about without symbols. Biblical food talk always, always points to great truths.

Psalm 104 is a beaut! It credits the King of Israel with the creation of all things for the delight of man- and womankind. Now be careful, since the Bible also tells us that we are totally responsible for what the creator has given us. We are not to misuse it! Adam even has the responsibility of naming the animals, and of taking care of them. In any case here are the lines that will help us get into the issue:

> Thou dost cause the grass to grow for the cattle,
>> and plants for man and woman to cultivate,
> that they may bring forth food from the earth,
>> and wine to gladden the heart of man and woman,
> oil to make their faces to shine,
>> and bread to strengthen their hearts.
>>
>> Psalm 104:14–15

The images of bread and wine and oil certainly don't do much for us in our culture but in the ancient world you were talking about reality!

Ben Sirach, in the Apocrypha, a collection of early manuscripts of the Biblical period which were never canonized, or included in the formal Bible, tells us that the normal diet of the peoples of ancient Palestine consisted of bread, salt, olive oil, olives, wine, and on a good day some dried fish. Red meat was eaten only on High Holy Days or special feasts. So, given that information, let us look at the diet and what the Bible is really talking about.

BREAD TO STRENGTHEN
THEIR HEARTS

The Psalmist claims that bread is to strengthen our hearts. Since bread was the most common part of the meal every day we can be sure that he is talking about something other than just plain bread. After all, the writer had no word for life-sustaining force, so he used bread for that classic symbol.

Consider what bread meant in the ancient world. Every day each Momma got up at about five in the morning and began baking bread. You had bread for three meals a day, and there were no Snack Packs! When a meal was ready, the whole family gathered and the junior high kids simply could not say that they would miss dinner because of basketball practice. You ate bread with the family or you did not eat at all. That was it.

We do not understand bread as a necessity in our time because in our time bread has become an addendum. In the old days Momma would put out the bread along with a few side dishes and she would say, "Do you suppose that anyone would want something else?" In our time we kill an entire cow, cook her, and place her on the buffet. Then Momma asks, "Do you suppose someone will want bread?" Bread is an addendum in our time, it is not a basic necessity at all, and we are poorer for it.

Bread was so important in the Old World that it was used as the word for "life." Indeed, the Hebrew word for bread, *Lechem,* means food in general and thus life itself. Without bread you were dead. Dead!

Manna from Heaven, or "Grain from Heaven," was also a symbol for the fact that no matter what kind of a jam we get ourselves into, the Holy One will be there ahead of us, along with manna from Heaven that we probably do not deserve.

Bread and grain are also used in the Bible to teach us about our responsibility to our fellow men and women. "Do not harvest the whole of the field, but leave the corners for the wandering hungry that will come by" (Deuteronomy 24:19). So why is the farmer responsible for the hungry? Because he has grain, and he must not keep it all for himself. Bread teaches us that we must feed each other or some of us will die.

There are wonderful ways in which bread is used to point away from itself to the fact that we are dependent upon God's good Creation. The Psalms refer to the Bread of the Angels, and the Bible talks of the Bread of Affliction, the Bread of Toil, and the Bread of Tears. Bread was a perfect symbol for our life as those who must struggle and toil and still remain faithful to the Holy One.

The word for bread in Hebrew also refers to our dependence on one another for community and life support. To this day kosher bakers offer a prayer before they bake the challah, or traditional egg bread. As a matter of fact, all Orthodox Jewish Grandmas offer the same prayer. A tiny bit of dough is removed from the whole of the batch and it is thrown onto the floor of the hot oven. As the smoke from the dough rises to heaven one is to pray for those who are hungry.

Can we decide not to eat bread? No, if we do not eat we die, and thus we confess that we are not God. We are totally, totally dependent upon the Creator. Without bread we are not. So, in the eating of bread we see the destruction of dualistic camps in theology that claim we are half God and half man. No, we eat of God's Creation or we die. We are certainly not in charge here!

Finally, this whole concept of bread as a life symbol was carried into the Latin Church. In Latin the term for "companion" (*companio*) refers to bread. *Com* (with) and *panis* (bread) means "The person with whom I break my bread. My companion." From this concept we gain insight into the New Testament phrase "He was known in the breaking of the Bread."

Biblical talk about bread is not about bread at all, but rather about our total dependence upon the Creator and upon one another.

OIL TO MAKE OUR FACE SHINE

Fatness is certainly not a popular thing in our time. Everyone is trying to cut down on fat and I am sure that peoples in the Old World would wonder what is going on in our culture. The Jews spent many generations in the desert literally starving to death, so fatness became a symbol of joy. No, one was not expecting to get fat on his own, but surely a time would come in which we would celebrate fatness as a people. Remember, everything in the Bible is always communal, rarely private.

To a people who had so few universals in their language, fatness was the perfect image for that time in which we would no longer want. We would be fat as a people.

Proverbs offers "Blessed [read happy] is he who drips with fatness." This line refers to the end of hunger, and not just physical hunger but spiritual hunger as well. One hungers and thirsts for the righteousness of the Lord . . . and fatness means fulfillment.

In Isaiah 55 the prophet looks to a time in which we can

"delight ourselves in fatness." We can delight ourselves in fulfillment as members of the human community. I really love this image though it seems to scare the daylights out of followers of the Protestant Work Ethic. Relax. Enjoy that which God has given us. Enjoy Creation, His gift to us, in excess. Delight yourselves in fatness.

And how did this fatness cause our face to shine? In Biblical times an oily face was a symbol of joy. It meant that you were well fed and quite pleased with yourself. When these early peoples went to a party they rubbed olive oil upon their faces so that they might look shiny and happy. Oil on the face reflects light, and since light has its source in the Creator, by rubbing oil upon your face you would increase your countenance and your ability to reflect light. Further, they could always rub goat fat under their armpits so that when they danced with joy they would not smell. Are you getting this?

The Protestant Ethic has taught us that we are always to be in control of our emotions, thus fatness is looked down upon in our culture as a sign of someone who has lost control. Further, we would never put oil upon our face before going to a party since we know that when your face is oily your emotions can be seen right away! One little wince of an oily face and all can see how you feel. So, since we are to always be in total control of our emotions we would never oil our faces. No, before we go to a party we powder our face down! This hides and masks any emotional twinge that might be seen by those around us.

Not so in the Bible. Fatness in the Bible, at least fatness of the community, was a sign of our enjoyment of the wonders of Creation, of the fact that God loves us and seeks fulfillment for us. There will be a time when hunger, both of the spirit and of the stomach, will be no more. Blessed is he who drips with fatness! We can put oil upon our faces and dance to the wisdom of the Creator.

Fatness in the Bible is just wonderful and it is an act of celebration, not an act of lack of discipline. I have had enough discipline. The Holy One wants me to oil my face, and I do it often.

WINE TO GLADDEN OUR HEARTS

Let us deal with the old problem of whether in early times they actually drank wine as we know it—or was it just grape juice?

It was not grape juice. Grapes are one of the Creator's most clever inventions since there is yeast on the outside of the skin and sugar on the inside. Who else could have thought up such a package? All one has to do is crush the grape, and, according to R. F. Capon, "the juice goes on its God-given course to become wine. Indeed, something underhanded has to be done to grape juice in order to prevent it from going to fulfillment as God intended" (see Bibliography). That underhanded bit was used on grape juice in this country in the early days of Prohibition when the Welch family put pasteurized grape juice on the market so that the Methodist Church could still celebrate the Communion without wine. Incidentally, a leading member of the family was one of our bishops, Bishop . . . Welch. All sounds rather odd, doesn't it?

In any case, we know that grape fermentation was common in Biblical times. I will admit that the wine was probably pretty green, since only the very wealthy could afford wine that was imported and aged. The normal Hebrew family drank pretty informal stuff, but it was wine nevertheless.

The Biblical writers chose wine as the classic symbol of joy. Wine is to make our hearts glad, and it works very well. Drunkenness is always condemned in the Biblical community but wine is to be shared as a communal symbol of joy.

I hope you can attend contemporary Sabbath Eve services at your local temple. The Jewish Sabbath Eve begins with the most wonderful question. Actually, it is only the answer that is given. Everyone knows the question, but it is never stated. Jews would never bother with such nonsense. Everyone knows that the question is "Just how clever and glorious is this image of the Creator that you are now about to worship?" Rather than actually state the question the service begins with the answer. A Kiddush cup is raised and the service beings with this blessing: "Blessed art thou, Lord God, King of the Universe, Creator of the fruit of the vine!" There, that is how clever the Creator is.

In ancient times one could never have a service of celebration or thanksgiving without wine. Therefore, the first thing that Noah did when the Ark finally hit solid ground was to shout to the crew that they were to land and plant the vines. Since vines take about seven years before they produce grapes for wine we can assume that Noah and his friends waited about for seven years before they had the landing party.

Closer to our time it was Ben Franklin who said, "Wine is sure proof that God loves us and wants us to be happy."

Wine is to gladden our hearts, and I suppose we could have gotten along without it, but then, who would want to? The Creator is loving beyond all sense of reason. So, wine becomes a symbol of God's Creativity and Love, and in the end it turns out to be our oldest and best medicine.

A Few More Food Symbols

MUSHROOMS

I have always loved the mushroom as a symbol of the cleverness of the Creator. After all, mushrooms grow out of the waste and ruin of the cow or horse field. They grow from dead leaves and horse dung! Who else but the Holy One could come up with something as clever as that? Or as delicious?

Yes, we still use manure for fertilizing mushrooms, though now we sterilize it first. I thought I had better tell you that so you would not stop eating this classic symbol of God's creativity.

ARTICHOKES

What a grand way to eat a thorny old thistle. That is what they are, thistles. You have to wonder about the person who first tried eating one as their appearance certainly does not promise the treasure that is finally offered.

YEAST

Have you ever thought about what our lives would be without yeast? We certainly would not even be, that is for sure. From yeast come bread and wine and cheese and yogurt and medicine and beer. There must be some other joys that come from yeast that I cannot think of at the moment, but in any case this food product has got to be one of the most clever inventions of the Holy One. All we did was discover it, and then learn to use it. In the Bible you could also use it in theological conversation. So food talk in the Bible is really God talk, or theology.

Nomads in the Desert

We must understand the meaning of the nomadic mind-set if we are to really understand how food functions as a theological symbol in the Bible.

The ancient Hebrews were nomads, following the herds and living off the foods that grew wild in the desert. Because of this precarious life and the dangers of wandering in the desert, nomads traveled in groups; each person would help protect the next for the sake of the survival of the tribe. Everything was shared, everything. Out of sheer necessity that sharing involved food. As a matter of fact one could not own food in the very early days as all food was used for the sake of the whole of the community. If one person were to own the food and hold out on the rest of the tribe he would soon find himself alone in the midst of the wilderness.

The term *wilderness* points to the problem of the nomadic lifestyle. It was dangerous to wander about in the desert and so the nomadic peoples saw the inherent worth in each individual as a member of that protecting community. One's real value did not stem from what one could produce or own, but rather from the fact that one was a member of the tribe, a member of the community. In our culture we see value in the person only as he is productive. In ancient Israel the individual was valuable because he belonged.

In tribal or nomadic communities, when a person was asked to identify himself he gave his tribal name first. "I am a child of the God of Abraham, Isaac, and Jacob." Then perhaps a family name would be offered. In our culture when one asks us who we are, we begin by offering our first name. Then we go on to our family name. Then we tell the questioner what we do for a living. Everything was communal, not private, as in our system.

STARVATION

Starvation and hunger were daily problems of the nomadic life on the desert; and it was quite a regular event. Surely hunger can symbolize both the physical and spiritual lack of fulfillment in one's life: the lack of direction, and simply the lack of food. The confession of hunger is probably our first theological lesson, a lesson learned when we were very young. To know hunger is to know that we are in a precarious position, and that we are totally dependent upon someone or something apart from ourselves to ensure our survival on every level of our lives.

That first confession of our real condition hits each of us when we are very young. I eat of God's Creation or I die! That's all there is to it. I cannot get along on my own. I must have the help of others around me. I am not God. I am a child of Creation.

Nobody knew this confession better than those who wandered the desert in early times. This problem held the Hebrew nomads together as a community and defined their worth as protectors and members of the rest of the tribe.

RULE OF HOSPITALITY

Since the Hebrew nomads could not own food, and since food had to be shared for the sake of all, there arose on the desert the Rule of Hospitality. While it is not defined clearly in Scripture, it is referred to many times and in many ways. Everyone knew the Rule of Hospitality just as they all knew images that referred to shepherding.

This rule is terribly important to our understanding food and theology.

The Rule of the Desert is simple. If you are in camp on the desert and a stranger wanders into your camp he must be fed, no matter how little food you have. But if he is an enemy, he eats by himself in the corner!

Here we see the meaning of the table in the Bible. The concrete language of the people of Israel had few words that referred to community. That was too general a term. We are lucky that they had a word for family! But they did have the concept of the table. In short, the Rule of Hospitality means that whenever you were at table there could be no enemies present. Not one. So eventually being at table with another person meant that you were saying to that person that you could not and would not ever see him or her as an enemy. The table became the place for the celebration of all pacts, promises, and real intimacy. To be at table with someone in Biblical times was to be more intimate than being with them in bed! Eating together was the fullest and most important symbol of intimate sharing.

This rule for table was observed even in the royal household. It would work like this: The King is at table entertaining some local big shots. A member of the King's staff enters and whispers to the King, "Lord, you have a traitor at the table." Now, if the King had been a ruler in Babylonia, or Phoenicia, or even in Saudi Arabia in our time, all he needed to say was "Take him out and cut his head off." No trial, no questions. This was done in Saudi Arabia just a few years ago. But this King, he was a King of Israel. So, he would simply stand and point to the enemy and say, "I will not eat with you!" All would rise and this enemy would have to leave not only the table, but the town as well. One did not eat with enemies.

On the other hand, to offer food to someone was to engage in the most wonderful communication imaginable. Remember that Abraham was visited by the Lord in the form of three angels (Genesis 18). They came in the midst of the noonday nap and awoke Abraham, the father of the faith. Abraham was startled to

Rembrandt's *Abraham Feeding the Angels*

see three strangers, yet he brought water so that they might wash their feet and he ordered his wife to start baking bread. He then ran to the fields to fetch a calf for roasting. This unexpected lunch must have taken several hours to prepare. He then sat with them and watched as they ate beneath a shade tree. He had never seen these people before in his life and they had actually come on behalf of the Lord. Such is the Rule of Hospitality.

Biblical View of Community

Food functioned in the Bible as a means of communication, and the table became the symbol of intimacy. Indeed, eating with someone at table was considered more intimate than sexual involvement. (Although I must tell you that during all the years that I functioned as a marriage counselor and chaplain I always urged my students and parishioners to build the bedroom right next to the kitchen!)

Since no enemies were to be at table with you, though you were expected to feed them in the corner, table language became theological language. In the Biblical account of Moses receiving the Ten Commandments, the Decalogue, we find a fascinating story. The story states that Moses went up onto the mountain to receive the Law of God. He stood there, amid the smoke that was a sign of the presence of the Holy One. Then he heard the sound of the trumpet, the Shophar, the ram's horn used to call the Hebrew people together. The scene is terribly powerful and Moses' followers are warned to not even look at the mountain. However, once the laws had been given, Moses returned from the mountain and he then took Aaron and some of the other elders back up to the mountain with him. After all of that smoke and awesome fear no one was harmed in the least. Indeed, they "ate and drank" with the King of the Universe (Exodus 24:11). Now that is intimacy!

It is hard for people in our culture to accept the intimacy of the table . . . well, actually it was a rug on the desert. In Biblical times when a meal was offered all had to be present. There were no Snack Packs, nor was there a freezer full of convenience foods. They had to take their meals with and confront the whole of the family at least three times a day, and this was a holy time, a time of intimacy.

The banquet table and feasting eventually became so important in ancient Israel that the prophets speak of the fulfillment of history in terms of a grand feast. In Isaiah 55, Deutero-Isaiah, sometimes called Second Isaiah, speaks of a time in which history will be fulfilled. And what will happen? All peoples of the Earth will gather at one table, all will eat with one another, and that means that there will be no enemies present. Everyone will be called upon to see all others as Children of God. Such a meal!

Cain and Abel

What could this odd Old Testament story have to do with food and theology? It is a perfect example of how food talk is actually God talk.

This story, while it is in Genesis, the first book of the Bible, was certainly not one of the first stories that the Children of Israel used to explain their history or their commitment to the Covenant. After all, Genesis talks about the beginnings, but the book was not put into its final form until after the establishment of the Kingdom, after the Jews had stopped their wanderings. It is very much like our own understanding of our history. We really do not understand our youth until we are old enough to look back and put things together. So it is with Jewish history. They look back in order to explain what is going on in the current time, and to point to the future. I suppose that is what history is supposed to do, and the Children of Israel did it well.

This is obviously a story from a later time because Cain had a farm. He had stopped wandering and he drew his livelihood from his private property. Abel, his brother, was not a tiller of the soil but a keeper of sheep, a common image of the communal life, of the life that the prophets claimed we were called to by the Holy One. Sheep are communal by their very nature. As a matter of fact we do not even have a word for one sheep. The term is always understood to be plural. Further, a shepherd was simply the keeper of the sheep, not necessarily the owner. The sheep belonged to the community that hired the shepherd.

So we have two very different life-styles here. One belongs to the communal man who must share the desert and nomadic values to which the old prophets were calling people to return, and the other belongs to a private property owner who shared his crops only upon payment.

It is obvious which life-style the prophet claimed to be the choice of the Lord of Israel. Each of the brothers brought a sacrifice to the Holy One, Cain's gift coming from his private crops and Abel's gift being a newborn lamb. The Lord accepted Abel's gift but he rejected Cain's gift, without explanation. We don't need an explanation. These gifts were symbolic of the private landowner over against the communal man who had to share everything, just as did the nomads. So when Cain's gift was rejected, "his countenance fell." He was so angry that he took Abel out into the field and killed him. His blood seeped into Cain's own soil and then Cain was confronted by the Holy One. "Where is Abel, your brother?" Cain offers one of the most impudent and nasty remarks in the entire Bible. He replies, "Hey, don't get put out. Am I my brother's keeper?" Thus we see the two life-styles.

In order to teach Cain about His intentions for men and women as children of God, Cain is condemned to wander forever. In that wandering he would finally come to see that the values of the Bible stem from our understanding that we are really nomads, wanderers, and we are to care for and protect one another, not just our property.

Slavery among the Children of Israel did not occur while they were on the desert, of course. It did not begin until the Kingdom was established and the people could become landowners rather than people of the desert.

It is interesting to note that while we know of the death of Abel, and of most other characters in the Bible, we know nothing of the death of Cain. Is he still around? I have always thought that the phrase "Looters will be shot" is very much a Cain phrase.

Feasting as Commitment

In the Bible the table is regarded as the most serious place for significant relationships. Since no enemies could be present at the table, taking one's place at the table was itself a commitment to peace. The table was the symbol used to represent the healing of history.

The 23rd Psalm says it beautifully, though we are always so anxious to get through the valley of the shadow of death that we neglect a major portion of the Psalm. "The Lord prepares a table in the presence of mine enemies." Good heavens, that was against the law. You could not eat with your enemies, and there was certainly no way that you were going to put out a table for them.

But the Lord, that's different.

The Lord prepares the banquet table that heals the rifts between enemies. We cannot; the risks are too great, the plotting too intense. When we throw a dinner party we invite only like-minded people—we need that control. "Well, we've got to invite the Burchams, we owe them one. Boy, are they boring! And listen, dear wife, if you invite Gail and that friend of hers I'm leaving the house. They will fight all night and ruin our party."

We want to be in control . . . and thus we create feasts based on a phoney world, a world in which we do not have to reach out to others—no enemies, not even people who might make us feel uncomfortable.

Not so with the King of the Universe.

The Lord prepares a table in the presence of our enemies and thus we are all obligated to sit with one another, to pass over our differences, since we are all the beloved of God. We are talking difficulty here and it is obvious that only the Lord can prepare such a table. You and I have not the nerve, let alone the inclination or the patience. But the Holy One demands that we get along with one another.

The Feast was so necessary to the forming of common bonds and agreements that we see a tie between the meaning of the term *Feast* and the term *Covenant*. Never was a covenant formed in Biblical times without a feast to seal it. Weddings, baptisms, circumcisions, the return of the wayward child, all called for a feast. I have officiated at many weddings in my time and I always check on the reception table. When I see nothing but a bowl of candy-covered almonds and a few chopped-ham open-face sandwiches I think, "I'll give this marriage three weeks, max." Where is the feast, the joy, the celebration of the joining of two families and a hundred strangers?

Food consumed communally, as understood in Biblical times, made you a member of the same family or tribe. I suppose we understand this today when we say, "Stay and eat. You're just like family!" But for the people of the desert this was no warm and charming invitation. They were absolutely serious, and thus you became not only a part of the family but also a part of its traditions and with that its responsibilities.

Who was the enemy in Biblical times? It was anyone who stood against the Laws and Will of Yahweh, the Lord of Israel. It was anyone who was of a foreign tribe who did not take to the Covenant or to the Laws of Moses. It was anyone who had become a tax collector or a prostitute or an adulterer. In short, it could very well be most of the people that you knew. All must be brought to a common table and thus a common feast. There could be no enemies there.

Soul as Appetite

One of the most beautiful images of food talk as God talk in the Bible comes from the meaning of hunger. The word for *soul* in Hebrew does not mean at all what it came to mean in medieval theology. In medieval times the word *soul*, with its Hellenistic background, meant that each person had a spark of God within him, a seed, or the idea that the Creator had planted a seed within the human form. The seed goes on to fulfillment, bringing the desire of the Creator to completion. "Great oaks from little acorns grow" is a very Hellenistic statement.

In the Hebrew Bible there is no notion that God implants the soul that makes man half God. No such implications whatsoever. The Hebrew word translated as "soul" refers to "appetite." What are you hungry for? Your appetite either craves the Law of the Lord or the life of the flesh.

> As a hart longs
> for flowing streams,
>   so longs my soul
>   for thee, O God.
> My soul thirsts for God,
>   for the living God.
>   Psalm 42: 1-2 (See also Psalm 63:1.)

We are not half god and half man, as the Hellenists claim, but rather we are children of God, as the Bible claims, and we certainly have a lot of childish hungers. Those hungers symbolize the real hungers that one encounters in this world.

The yearning to fulfill our hunger, our soul, as God's people was brought to the sacrificial altar. The practice of offering sacrifices was common at the Temple in Biblical times and appeared to be a holdover from the pagan world. However, the Jews, unlike the pagans, were never acting as if they were offering sacrifices to an unknown and unreasonable god, but rather, as I see it, they were attempting to offer a meal to the Creator, to Feast with the One from whom we feel separated. It was an attempt to establish the most holy dinner table, with all of us being present before the Lord as Host.

The Passover Seder

The Hebrew language must be very creative when communicating universals, as the language has few. So, as we have said before, in order to discuss those matters which are of supreme importance, one does not gossip in philosophical language. Rather, one symbolizes and tells stories.

Thus the Seder meal of Passover.

I know of no celebration in the Hebrew tradition that more clearly points to the notions behind this book. *Jews do not discuss theology so much as eat it!*

Throughout the Seder, the Hebrew speaks in the first person as if the one who is reading was present. That is how the service is read and that is how we must think.

The meal is full of references to the historical flight to freedom when we ran from Egyptian captivity. After all, we had been in Egypt since Joseph brought us there seeking grain for bread, and that was four hundred years before. A new Pharaoh came to power and turned us into slaves. Moses arose and was favored in the royal household, until he found out that he was actually a member of the Hebrew tribes. You will remember that he stood firm with our people and defied the Pharaoh, demanding that our people be set free. When the Pharaoh refused, Moses organized all the Children of the Hebrews and we made the great break for freedom.

Prior to our fleeing Egypt we were also saved from the plague called upon the people of Egypt. The angel of death "passed over" our doors, another insight into the meaning of the Passover.

The events of the flight to freedom and the journey to the land of Canaan are recounted in the Seder meal, and everything is brought forth in detail by foods symbolic of the happenings. What a wonderful way to talk!

The food items point away from themselves to something beyond themselves, the calling of the people of Israel to flee and accept their place as a people chosen to bear a very profound and awesome responsibility.

The table is set with the best serving pieces that the family can afford. The whole of the house has been cleansed so that no remaining flour from the previous season can infect the new flour of this joyous time of liberation and insight. Fresh matzo is made by certified bakers so that all know the new bread is fresh and clean and that the flour and water have not been in contact for more than eighteen minutes, at which time it might rise; rising is not permitted. If any dishes needing flour are prepared during Passover, the flour must be made from finely ground new matzo. Now, everything is ready for the service. It is held in the home and it is a major event in the life of every Jew.

Several food items, which are now theological history pieces, are on the table. The matzo, which we learned to bake on the desert without leavening, is there. Moses warned us that we would be running so fast that dough would not have the time to rise, so he told us to leave behind the leavening that we had brought into Egypt. It was a type of sourdough that we had learned to bake on the desert. We left it behind and a generation later the Egyptians announced that they had learned to bake the very first leavened barley cake. They learned it from us, the Jews! To this day the matzo is eaten during Passover in order to make present again Moses' call for us to be ready to move when the Holy One calls. The service calls it "The Bread of Affliction," but I refer to matzo as "The Bread of Hustle."

A story I must tell you. It is perfectly all right to interrupt the narrative of the flight with a story from your own family. Indeed, the Haggadah, the book of service for the Seder meal, claims that he who embellishes upon the stories of the journey is blessed and to be admired. So, this story.

Matzos are not particularly tasty. After all, they are not supposed to be. They are symbolic of that time of toil and oppression when we were running across that desert trying to escape from our captors!

I have conducted many Seders for Protestant churches. One evening I had the University of Puget Sound Chapel filled with bright young students who were anxious to better understand Hebrew traditions. Rabbi Richard Rosenthal helped me conduct the event. When it came time to taste and share a major symbol in the meal, which is really a matzo, I offered it to the rabbi. He was to bless it and distribute it. Since it was not Passover season I could not find real Passover matzo, so I bought several boxes of daily matzos, egg and onion matzos. The rabbi bit into the egg and onion matzo and quietly spit it out. "These will not do for Passover, Jeff. These are delicious!"

Another dish on the table is charoses. Made from ground apples, red wine, cinnamon, sugar, and perhaps walnuts, this paste looks very much like mortar, and this is precisely how it is to appear. It is to make present all of the mortar that we heaped brick upon brick when we were slaves in Egypt. Rather than discuss the philosphical meaning of slavery and captivity, one places charoses, the mud of captivity, on the matzo, the bread of hustle, and one eats this sandwich of freedom. You eat it!

During the meal one also tastes of a bowl of salt water, making present the tears that we shed during the trek to the new land. There is a bitter herb on the plate, usually horseradish, to help us deal with the bitter things that happened during the trip. There is also a sweet herb—parsley is fine for this—to make us mindful of all of the sweet things that happened during the journey.

A hard-boiled egg, roasted or rolled over a fire or stove-top burner, makes present the many sacrifices that were offered on our behalf at the altar in earlier times. Finally, there is a roasted lamb shank bone making present the remains of the Paschal lamb that was offered in earlier times and was eaten the night of the Passover. You may read more about the nature of the image of the blood of the lamb on page 59.

The whole of this wonderful service is conducted in the first person. It is not a bit of memory work but rather the actual celebration of the meaning of history in the present tense. I will never forget my Protestant students in Introduction to Religion classes turning to the one or two token Jews we had in the class. "How can your father read, 'When I was a slave in Egypt the Lord led me out with a strong hand and a mighty arm'? Your father has never been in Egypt!" The Jewish student seemed always to respond in the same way. "I don't understand your question!" Such is a present and real understanding of history, of those events that shape our present and our future.

I recall one semester when I was offering a seminar on Death and Dying. It was a very new course for the sixties and Jack Markovitz, a charming guy from Los Angeles, enrolled. Each student in this small class was to take a day for the presentation of his or her semester paper. One student did a study on how men versus women commit suicide. Another talked about death as a frontier symbol in American literature. All of these papers were deep and dark and fascinating. On the day that Jack was to read his paper he began with an introduction to the Passover Seder. He then took us through the entire Haggadah. He read the whole works! In a class on Death and Dying? I was really wondering where he could possibly be leading us when he concluded with the final prayer of the Seder feast. At that point, according to his narrative, the daughter of the reader climbed up into his lap and whispered, "You read the service just as well as Grampa did!" Grampa had died just before the Seder, and this was the young man's first time to read in the present tense, "When I was a slave in Egypt, the Lord led me out with a strong hand and a mighty arm!"

The Seder is beyond the death of all of us. Markovitz received an A for the semester.

The following service is a gift to us from the congregation of

Temple Beth-El in Tacoma, Washington. They provided this for my University Chapel students during the late sixties. It will work well in your own home or in your local church just prior to Easter. (Most Biblical scholars agree that Jesus was celebrating the Seder meal about the time of the Last Supper.)

My instructions for you are in parenthesis.

A family of four to eight is seated around the common table. If you do this in a local church, put a table in the center of the room with a chosen family. The rest of us can sit about the room, about the table.

IMPORTANT: Remember to set a place for Elijah, the expected one. I usually put his place at the other end of the table, opposite the papa's chair. No one is expected to sit in this place . . . unless, of course, Elijah does appear this year. In such a case we wish to be ready and welcoming to this image of the coming Messiah.

MODEL SEDER MEAL

WELCOMING THE PASSOVER WITH THE FESTIVAL OF LIGHTS BY THE MOTHER

The mother lights the candles at the table.

Praised art Thou, O Lord our God, Ruler of the universe. Thou hast sanctified us with Thy commandments and commanded us to kindle the holy day lights.

Praised art Thou, O Lord our God, Ruler of the universe. Thou hast given us life, kept us securely and brought us to this holy season.

KIDDUSH—SANCTIFICATION OF THE FESTIVAL

The leader (Papa) lifts the wine cup and prays:

Praised art Thou, O Lord our God, King of the universe, Thou has called us and sanctified us with Thy commandments. Lord, our God, out of love Thou didst give us festivals for happiness, holy days and seasons of joy; this Passover season, our festival of freedom. This holy assembly is called together to remember the exodus from Egypt.

Thou hast chosen us for Thy service and given us holy days for joy and happiness. Praised art Thou, O Lord, who dost bless Israel and the festivals.

Praised art Thou, O Lord our God, Ruler of the universe, Creator of the fruit of the vine.

(All drink a bit of the wine and toast the Holy One. Yes, even the children are to have a little glass with a little wine.)

CARPAS—BLESSING THE SPRING GREENS

Parsley or other salad greens, distributed to all, are dipped in salt water, and eaten after reciting the blessing.

Praised art Thou, O Lord our God, Ruler of the universe, Creator of the produce of the earth.

YACHAZ—DIVIDING THE MIDDLE MATZO

The middle one of the three matzos in the Passover plate is broken. One half is left on the plate; the other, called "afikomen," is hidden to be eaten at the end of the meal.

(The meal cannot be concluded until the afikomen is found. Where is it? It was given to the youngest member of the family, who hid it. He will produce it only after he has talked his grandfather into a trip to Disneyland, or a new bicycle, or . . . well, you get the picture. I have seen uncles and aunts and grandparents bid on the afikomen in order to close the evening. All the youngest has to do is sit there until he gets what he wants. It's beautiful!)

MAGID—TELLING THE PASSOVER STORY

The leader (Papa) lifts up the matzos and says:

Behold the bread of affliction which our fathers ate in Egypt. Let all who are hungry come and eat. Let all who are in need come and celebrate the Passover with us. May it be God's will to redeem us from all trouble and from all slavery. Next year at this season, may the whole house of Israel be free.

THE FOUR QUESTIONS

The youngest person at the table asks:

Why is this night different from all other nights? On all other nights, we eat either leavened or unleavened bread. Why on this night do we eat only unleavened bread?

On all other nights we may eat any kind of greens; why on this night must we taste bitter greens?

On all other nights we need not dip any food in another, even once; why on this night must we dip greens twice, the salad greens in salt water and the bitter herb in charoses?

On all other nights we may eat either sitting upright or at ease; why on this night are we all at ease? (Here the child refers to the fact that everyone in the family has a cushion on their chair. In the old world a cushion was the mark of a free man. A slave never sat on a cushion!)

WE CELEBRATE TONIGHT BECAUSE . . .

The father answers the child:

We were Pharaoh's slaves in Egypt. But the Lord our God rescued us, with a mighty hand and an outstretched arm. If He had not brought our fathers out of Egypt, then we and our children and our children's children might still be enslaved to Pharaoh in Egypt. Therefore, even if all of us were men of understanding, ripe in age and wisdom, and well versed in Torah, it would still be our duty each year to repeat the story of the exodus from Egypt. And the man who enjoys elaborating on the story of that liberation is a man to be admired.

THE FOUR SONS

On the subject of Passover, Scripture speaks of four types of human beings. (Choose any one of the family children to play any one of these roles.)

The **intelligent** son asks: "What is the meaning of all the Passover customs and ceremonies, the rules and rites which God has commanded?" (You will explain to him all the traditions of Pesach down to the last detail of the afikomen.)

The **wicked** son asks: "What's the sense of all this business of yours?" (*Yours*, he says, and none of *his*. By refusing to identify himself with the community he denies a basic principle of our religion. You may fling this in his teeth: "I do this because of what the Lord did for *me* when He rescued me from Egypt." *Me*, not *him*. If he had been there, he would not have been worthy of being saved.)

The **simple** son merely asks: "What is this?" Tell him: "With a strong hand, God took us out of Egypt where we were slaves."

And the son who is too **incompetent** even to inquire, get him started by quoting the words from the Bible: "In the day you shall tell your son saying (point to ceremonial dishes): All of this is because of what the Lord did for me when I came out of Egypt" (Exodus 13:14).

THE STORY OF THE OPPRESSION

Papa continues to read.

It is well for all of us, whether young or old, to consider how God's help has been our unfailing stay and support through ages of trial and persecution. Ever since He called our father Abraham from the bondage of idolatry to his service of truth, He has been our Guardian; for not in one country alone nor in one age have violent men risen up against us, but in every generation and in every land, tyrants have sought to destroy us; and the Holy One, blessed be He, has delivered us from their hands.

The Torah tells us that when Jacob our father was a homeless wanderer, he went down into Egypt, and sojourned there few in number. All the souls of his household were threescore and ten. And Joseph was already in Egypt; he was the governor over the land. And Joseph placed his father and his brethren, and gave them a possession, as Pharaoh had commanded. And Israel dwelt in the land of Goshen; they got them possessions therein, and were fruitful, and multiplied exceedingly.

And Joseph died, and all his brethren, and all that generation. Now there arose a new king over Egypt, who knew not Joseph. And he said unto his people: "Behold, the people of the children of Israel are too many and too mighty for us; come let us deal wisely with them, lest they multiply, and it come to pass that when war befalleth us anywhere, they also join themselves unto our enemies and fight against us, and get them up out of our land." Therefore they set over them taskmasters to afflict them with burdens. And they built for Pharaoh store cities, Pithom and Ramses. But the more the Egyptians afflicted them, the more the Israelites multiplied and the more they spread abroad.

The Egyptians dealt ill with us, and afflicted us, and laid upon us cruel bondage. And we cried unto the Lord, the God of our fathers, and the Lord heard our voice and saw our affliction and our toil and our oppression. And the Lord brought us forth out of Egypt, with a mighty hand and with outstretched arm and with great terror and with signs and with wonders. He sent before us Moses and Aaron and Miriam. And He brought forth his people with joy, His chosen ones with singing. And he guided them in the wilderness, as a shepherd his flock.

Therefore He commanded us to observe the Passover in its season, from year to year, that His law shall be in our mouths, and that we shall declare His might unto our children, His salvation to all generations.

All pray in unison: Who is like unto Thee, O Lord, among the mighty? Who is like unto Thee, glorious in holiness, fearful in praises, doing wonders? The Lord shall reign for ever and ever.

DAYENU

The company repeats the refrain "dayenu" which is equivalent to "It would have satisfied us."

Had He brought us out of Egypt and not divided the sea for us,

DAYENU

Had He divided the sea, and not permitted us to cross on dry land,

DAYENU

Had He permitted us to cross the sea on dry land, and not sustained us for forty years in the desert,

DAYENU

Had He sustained us for forty years in the desert and not fed us with manna,

DAYENU

Had He fed us with manna and not given us the Sabbath,

DAYENU

Had He given us the Sabbath and not brought us to Mount Sinai,

DAYENU

Had He brought us to Mount Sinai, and not given us the Torah,

DAYENU

Had He given us the Torah, and not led us into the Land of Israel,

DAYENU

Had He led us into the Land of Israel, and not built for us the Temple,

DAYENU

Had He built for us the Temple, and not sent us prophets of truth,

DAYENU

Had He sent us prophets of truth, and not made us a holy people,

DAYENU

All: "How much more then are we to be grateful unto the Lord for the manifold favors He has bestowed upon us!"

THE PASSOVER SYMBOLS

Rabban Gamaliel used to say, "He who does not explain the three essential symbols of the Seder has not discharged his Passover duty." They are Pesach, the Paschal lamb; matzo, the unleavened bread; and moror, the bitter herbs.

One of the company asks: "What is the meaning of Pesach?"

The leader (Papa) lifts up the shank bone and answers:

Pesach means the Paschal lamb, and is symbolized by this shank bone. It was eaten by our fathers while the Temple was in existence, as a memorial of God's favors, as it is said: "It is the sacrifice of the Lord's Passover, for that He passed over the houses of the children of Israel in Egypt, when He smote the Egyptians and delivered our houses" (Exodus 12:27). As God in ancient "Watch-Night" passed over and spared the houses of Israel, so did He save us in all kinds of distress, and so may He always shield the afflicted, and forever remove every trace of bondage from among the children of man.

One of the company asks: "What is the meaning of matzo?"

The leader lifts up the matzo and answers:

Matzo, called the Bread of Affliction, was the hasty provision that our fathers made for their journey, as it is said: "And they baked unleavened cakes of the dough which they brought out of Egypt. There was not sufficient time to leaven it, for they were driven out of Egypt and could not tarry, neither had they prepared for themselves any provisions" (Exodus 12:39). The bread which of necessity they baked unleavened thus became a symbol of divine help.

One of the company asks: "And what is the meaning of moror?"

The leader lifts up the bitter herbs and answers:

Moror means bitter herbs. We eat it in order to recall that the lives of our ancestors were embittered by the Egyptians, as we read: "And they made their lives bitter with hard labor in mortar and bricks and in all manner of field labor. Whatever task was imposed upon them, was executed with the utmost rigor" (Exodus 1:14). As we eat it in the midst of the festivities of this night, we rejoice in the heroic spirit which trials developed in our people. Instead of becoming embittered by them, they were sustained and strengthened.

In every generation it is each man's duty to look upon himself as if he personally had come out of Egypt. For we are commanded: "Tell your son in that day that it is because of what the Lord did for me when I came out of Egypt" (Exodus 13:8). It was not only our fathers whom God saved; He saved us also along with them.

HALLEL. Psalms 113 and 114 are read.

THE SECOND CUP OF WINE

The wine cup is raised.

Praised art Thou, O Lord, Ruler of the World, Who redeemed us when He redeemed our fathers from Egypt, and brought us to this night on which we eat matzo and bitter herbs. So mayest Thou, Lord God of our fathers, bring us ever in peace to the celebration of other holy days and festivals. May we share joyously in work of bringing Thy salvation and may we find happiness in Thy service. Gratefully we will sing anew unto Thee for our freedom and for our lives which have been saved. Blessed art Thou, O Lord, Redeemer of Israel.

Praised art Thou, O Lord, Ruler of the universe, Who bringest forth food from the earth.

Praised art Thou, O Lord, Ruler of the universe, Thou hast made us holy with Thy commandments and commanded us to eat matzo.

BLESSING THE BITTER HERBS

Each Seder guest eats of the bitter herbs dipped in charoses after praying:

Praised art Thou, O Lord our God, Ruler of the universe, Thou hast made us holy with Thy commandments and commanded us to eat the bitter herb.

COMBINING THE SEDER SYMBOL

All eat bitter herbs, matzo, and charoses together.

This is in memory of the custom introduced by Hillel in Temple days. He would put together a piece of the Passover lamb, matzo, and bitter herb and eat all three together, so as to do exactly what the Torah says about the Passover lamb: "They shall eat it upon matzo and bitter herb" (Numbers 9:11).

THE MEAL IS EATEN

(The Passover meal is as important to the fulfillment of the holiday as are prayers and blessing of the Seder. Here the family enjoys the many dishes of the season, depending on the background of the family. Jews are found all over the world and thus this part of the meals varies according to the dishes of a particular grandma and tradition. We have always enjoyed gefilte fish, tszimmes, and matzo ball soup. What a meal!)

SHARING OF THE AFIKOMEN

The afikomen is taken from its hiding place and eaten. This marks the end of the meal.

BLESSING OVER THE MEAL

The grace begins with Psalm 126 and continues:

Leader: Friends, let us thank the Lord.
Company: Praised be the name of God now and evermore.
Leader: May it please this company to thank God of whose food we have eaten.
Company: Let us praise Him of whose food we have eaten and by whose goodness we live.
All: Blessed be He and blessed be His name.

Praised art Thou, O Lord our God, Ruler of the universe. In Thy goodness Thou sustainest all the world. With grace, kindness, and compassion Thou givest food to all flesh. Thy mercy endures forever. Because of Thy great goodness we have not lacked food. May we never be in want of it. Thou art God, Provider and Benefactor of all, preparing nourishment for every living thing Thou hast created. Praised be Thou, O Lord, who providest food for all.

THE THIRD CUP OF WINE

Praised art Thou, O Lord our God, King of the universe, Creator of the fruit of the vine.

OPENING THE DOOR FOR ELIJAH

The door is opened for the beloved prophet of hope. This is done to renew the ancient hope and trust in God.

(This event is terribly profound. Generally a young child of the house goes to the door closest to the dining room and opens it to see if Elijah is to appear this year, indeed in this place. It is a very exciting moment and one always wonders, "Is this the night?")

During earlier times in medieval Europe, Jews very often kept their door open for the whole Seder meal so that those who passed by could see that the event was simply a family at table. There was all kinds of stupid talk about Jews needing the blood of Christian babies for the baking of matzo, and on and on.

I think the most wonderful event centering around the opening of the door that I can ever remember occurred one night when I asked a junior high kid, seated at the table in the middle of the church dining room, to go to the door. I had explained the importance of the moment and the sense of anticipation was high, very high. The lad went to the door, opened it, and peered out into the darkness. He then stepped out onto the porch. Finally, after what was only a moment but seemed to be many minutes, he returned to the dining room and walked to his place at the table. No one spoke. Finally I said quite loudly, "Well, is Elijah here?" He replied, "Well, not that I could see." I would give him an A in theology anytime.

THE HALLEL IS CONCLUDED

Psalms 115–118, Psalm 136.

THE FINAL CUP OF WINE

Praised art Thou, O Lord our God, Ruler of the universe, Creator of the fruit of the vine.

Give us happiness on this festival of matzos, for Thou art good and doest good to all. So we thank Thee for the good earth, and the fruit of the vine.

Praised art Thou, O Lord, for the land of the fruit of the vine.

Amen.

Hebrew Doctrine of Creation

The way the Hebrews viewed Creation certainly colored the language that they chose for the discussion. Everything was created, according to the old prophets, for our delight and enjoyment. Therefore Abraham, the father of the faith, claimed that he did not worship the power of the sun or the moon or even the stars. Rather he worshipped the Holy One, who created all of these things and hung them in the heavens for our enlightenment.

It follows then that everything in Creation points away from itself to the glory of God. We are to do the same. Paul Tillich called this an image of "a sacramental universe in which everything points away from itself to that which is beyond, but in the very pointing that thing participates in the power of that to which it points." So the heavens declare the glory of God, and somehow participate in that glory. Nothing in the universe has power in its own right but only insofar as it can point to the Creator. The Hebrews did not see a pantheistic universe in which all things are linked into the god forces. Far from it, everything in Creation was made by Him, and for His use. There was no dualism involved, no theory of two worlds. This is God's Creation.

The Babylonians had a very different image of creation and they pretty much had to create their own theory. The god Marduk would battle with the forces of chaos, thrashing about in the sea of disorder, and as long as he could keep the confusion in check reality would maintain. It is really a very exciting account. Then, this great stone god would be taken from the temple each year, scrubbed down, and carried back into the temple on the New Year. Everyone would cheer, except the crowds of people that had to carry this statue . . . they were exhausted! Isaiah is watching all of this from the hillside and he laughs at their labors. He quotes the Lord of Israel who exclaims:

"Even to your old age I am He,
  and to gray hairs I will carry you.
I have made, and I will bear;
  I will carry and will save."
                                    Isaiah 46:4

In contrast, the Hellenistic doctrine of creation, that of the later Greeks, is based on a pantheistic image in which everything has the power of creation within it and is called to some sort of fulfillment to a goal that is placed within, sort of like a seed. That is how we came up with the idea that man- and womankind are half god/half man. This dualistic system of belief always makes me think that the Holy One made some serious mistakes, death being the biggest one. It implies that at death we will be set free to show off our real nature, that of the godhead. Hebrew thinking knows of no such dualism, as we are children of God. No error here!

But according to the Bible, there is only one mighty force in

Creation and it is the Holy One. In Biblical thinking there is no source of power more mighty than the Holy One of Israel. In contrast to the god Marduk battling with chaos and disorder in the Babylonian creation myth, *Enuma Elish*, the Hebrew Bible quotes the Lord as saying, "Earth, be!" And it was. There is no opposition here, none whatsoever. He called forth everything without opposition. Thus the story of Creation according to Genesis is almost boring when compared to the great battle that Marduk and the minor gods had to contend with. There was no battle in Genesis as the Lord of Israel is above all. Therefore, the account of creation is told in a very matter-of-fact manner . . . no opposing forces. The story is told in absolute confidence. I like that!

There is one interesting story of an opposing force but it is not in the Genesis account. Mention is made of a Leviathan, the sea serpent of chaos, in Psalm 74 and Isaiah 27. However, this symbol of our fear of the depths of the sea is slain by the Holy One without any difficulty. A later rabbinic legend claims that the Holy One will simply "make a banquet for the righteous from the flesh of the Leviathan." Even the serpent of chaos will be served up as food at the hand of the Creator! No battle here, just a matter-of-fact confidence and a big meal!

I remember a student from a very fundamentalist branch of the Church enrolling at the University of Puget Sound, where I was chaplain. He came to me one day and told me that he thought his Old Testament professor did not believe what he was teaching since he was so matter-of-fact about it. He just listed the mighty acts of God and went on with the lecture. No emotion whatsoever. And the teacher was our rabbi in Tacoma, Rabbi Richard Rosenthal! To this day I do not think that the student realized that the best of rabbinic teaching is rather pedantic since it is offered in utter confidence.

MANNA AS COMMUNICATION

That sense of utter confidence in the ability of the Creator to protect us can be seen in the story of the manna in the desert. The Hebrews had been wandering to the new land and were starving. During the night small crystalline cakes appeared on the desert and they were edible. According to the text the tribes lived on manna for some time, all the while knowing that it was a gift from God. We do not have to ask what the stuff was in scientific terms, though it could have been locust or cicada droppings, which are filled with sugar, or the secretions from a desert bush called the tamarisk. It does not matter. The term "manna" comes from the Hebrew phrase *Man-Hu,* which means "What is it?" The point is that manna represented for the Children of Israel the fact that God would always provide.

True to human nature, the Hebrews were not satisfied with such bare sustenance during difficult times. We never are, are we? They had been wandering in the desert for a long time, years in fact, and they figured that they should receive a reward richer than manna.

> Now the rabble that was among them had a strong craving; and the people of Israel also wept again, and said, "O that we had meat to eat! We remember the fish we ate in Egypt for nothing, the cucumbers, the melons, the leeks, the onions, and the garlic; but now our strength is dried up, and there is nothing at all but this manna to look at."
>
> Numbers 11:4–6

You can almost hear them calling it "this damn manna!" Perhaps they had forgotten to whom they belonged and thus they could not feast on manna. It tasted like coriander cakes made with honey, according to the text. Later traditions from the Talmud, the commentaries of the rabbis, and later rabbinical stories, claimed that the manna had many flavors, depending upon one's condition in life. To the young men it tasted like bread, to the elderly it tasted like wafers made with honey, to sucklings it tasted like milk from their mother's breast, to the sick it tasted like fine flour mingled with honey, while for the heathen it tasted as bitter as linseed. In any case, they were tired of it and thought they deserved something better. So it is with all of us.

Proverbs and Food Talk

Just to further my point a bit I suggest we look at the book of Proverbs. This is a most fascinating collection of stories and pithy sayings that were used to educate the young. Many of these lessons were taught through metaphors of food. The Proverbs give no real facts that you should know, rather they were short sayings, called "mashals," that gave you a certain insight into the mind of the followers of this Biblical tradition.

For instance:

As clouds and winds without rain, so is he who boasts of gifts ungiven.

Proverbs 25:14

What a great use of the story which is not even a story! However, each of us remembers the times as a child when we have said, "Well, I was going to invite you to my birthday party!" Enough said.

The fool over against the wise man is a major theme in Proverbs. It is not that the wise man knows stuff, it is just that he understands and turns to the Law of the Holy One. The fool, on the other hand, is not stupid, it is just that he cannot get into the will of God. He refuses and the more he tries to live on his own the more he demonstrates his foolishness. Now, a favorite of mine:

As a dog returneth to his vomit, so doth a fool repeat his folly.

Proverbs 26:11

In order to pass on these pithy bits of insight food and eating images are common in Proverbs.

Eateth not the bread of idleness

Proverbs 31:27

nor drink the wine of violence.

Proverbs 4:17

The term *soul* in Hebrew refers to your appetite, not the Hellenistic seed of God within you. If your appetite, or soul, hungers for the righteousness of the Lord, you are wise, but if your soul hungers after the flesh you are a fool.

The idle soul shall suffer hunger.

Proverbs 19:15

To the hungry soul every bitter thing tastes sweet.

Proverbs 27:7

Images of feasting on wisdom and eating that honey which gives knowledge of wisdom are common in this tradition.

The righteous eateth to the satisfying of his soul (appetite): but the belly of the wicked shall want.

Proverbs 13:25

Whoever is of a merry heart has a continual feast.

Proverbs 15:15

Better is a dinner of herbs where love is present than a meal of fatted ox in the midst of hatred.

Proverbs 15:16

As you can see, food and eating function throughout the Bible as God talk, not food talk.

Kosher Food Laws

One more issue, that of the kosher food laws. I offer a few observations to help non-Jewish readers understand why these laws are important to Jews.

Leviticus 11:3–9 gives a whole list of restrictions concerning what one could eat in early Biblical times. Now, these laws make sense only if you accept the basis of the commandment. Non-Jews usually believe that the kosher laws pertain to cleanliness. That is close, but "fit to eat" or "properly prepared" is closer. The opposite word, *teref*, simply means "unfit to eat." But the real issue here is that one subscribes to the kosher laws for one reason. They were prescribed by the Holy One. Thus, observance of the kosher food laws is an act of devotion, rather than just an act of dietary restriction.

According to kosher laws, one is not to eat unclean animals or unclean creatures from the sea such as anything that does not have scales or fins. That eliminates all shellfish, crabs, and scaleless fish, all of which are bottom eaters and therefore unclean. They eat garbage. This rule is easy to understand.

The rule against pork is more difficult. Leviticus forbids the eating of any animal that does not chew its cud and does not have a parted hoof. How did this rule come about? Pork was forbidden but it could not have been because of trichinosis, a disease that we did not even name until 1916. There is something more at stake here.

Remember that all kosher rules eventually have something to do with one's commitment to the Covenant between God and mankind. If we accept the fact that we are to be the people who will show the Lord of Israel to be the one true God, then we cannot afford to get sick and thus shirk our responsibility. However, we are a people of the desert and therefore we are nomads. We travel and continue to learn that we are dependent upon one another. That is what it means to be God's people: That means that our food supply must be nomadic too; it must be able to graze off the local desert plants. Sheep, goats, camels, even cattle will go with us . . . but not the pig. He is too much like us; he will not move unless he gets grain and water. A pig will eat you out of tent and water. The Jews could not be burdened by the pig if they were to be ready to move, at any time.

I clearly remember explaining this insight of the anthropologists on a television show. I received a letter from a very committed and right wing Orthodox rabbi who claimed that I had blasphemed every Jew in America. I was just explaining the sensible background of the no-pork rule. He insisted that the rule is obeyed not because of some cockeyed anthropological reason but because of the commandment, "Thus saith the Lord." That is the issue. He then cursed me right and left and, I suppose, spat upon the letter.

I was really disturbed by his anger, but after a year of thinking about this I now realize that he was right. The law is obeyed because it is given by God. Adhering to the kosher laws is more an act of devotion than it is an act of eating.

Nevertheless, cleanliness is a part of the law along with a certain humanitarian approach to how we get our food from living creatures. For instance, cattle are not to be slaughtered in an unkind manner. A simple cut in the throat with a very sharp knife gives the animal a very quiet and sleepy death. Further, if the animal is not frightened, as we frighten animals in a slaughterhouse, the meat will not be filled with adrenaline and therefore will be much more edible.

Another humane concept stems from the rule that you are not to cook an animal in the milk of its mother. No sour cream in a beef stew! No mixing dairy products with meat products. In the midst of devotional fervor, some of these rules are pushed to the edge a bit. I received several letters criticizing my delicious recipe for noodle kugel, a dish in which I had mixed rendered chicken fat, or schmaltz, with cream. Incidentally, I received this recipe from a producer friend of mine in Chicago, who is Jewish, but only God knows when she was last in Temple. Maybe God has forgotten, too! In any case, the letters told me that I was not to mix milk with meat. Well, the rule about cooking a creature in the milk of its mother I understand, but I still do not understand how you can get milk from a chicken. However, this rule has become a matter of adherence to the kosher law, which makes it incumbent upon observant Jews to respect, and I must accept it as such. No more cream mixed with chicken fat!

Blood was also to be carefully washed from the meat before it was cooked, the reason being, as stated in Leviticus 17:14, "The life of all flesh is the blood thereof." Blood is life, therefore we do not eat it. It is also true that blood can carry disease.

The rules from Leviticus, then, urge us to see our special relationship with the animals that God has created, and we must treat them kindly even though we need to eat them. Indeed, during the Creation story in Genesis we are given full responsibility for caring for these creatures, even to naming them. We are also given responsibility for caring for all Creation. We have not been doing too well lately.

A Quick Summary

To summarize, food talk in the Bible is actually God talk, or theological talk. The Hebrew language is very concrete and therefore uses symbols, metaphors, or myths in order to talk about realities to which you cannot point. Food images were perfect for the Biblical mind. Wine, bread, oil, salt—all pointed to the wisdom of the Holy One and to the meaning of human relationships.

The nomadic life-style of the Children of Israel resulted in an ethic based on the necessity of sharing in the desert . . . or all would starve. Therefore the Rule of Hospitality stated that one had to feed any stranger who wandered into the camp, but if this person was an enemy he ate in the corner by himself. To eat with someone therefore became a most serious symbol of community. To eat with a family meant you became a part of the group, sharing its hopes and insights. To be at table with someone was the most intimate relationship possible, even more intimate than that of the bedroom.

The Biblical view of community centered around the table. No covenant was formed without a feast to seal the pact, and the soul, or appetite, was fed as one came to understand his or her place as a child of the Creator.

Finally, the Bible uses all kinds of symbols, particularly food symbols, that point away from themselves to the cleverness of the Holy One.

New Testament
Table Manners

Jesus knew all of the preceding Hebrew traditions. Given the nature and commitments of his devoted parents, he knew the Scriptures very well. We also know he was trained as a rabbi. I don't believe that he had any mystical insight into some secret meaning of the Scriptures since his preaching was very plain, to the point, and rooted in the writings of the Prophets. But he did have a different understanding of history!

Jesus understood very well the rule about not eating with one's enemies, and since he was a devout Jew the enemies were very plain. No tax collectors, prostitutes, Samaritans, divorced women, you know the crowd. The rule of the day was simple. Avoid all of these people and see them as outside of the Kingdom of God.

Jesus, however, begins to preach to and teach these very people who are estranged; he is even seen eating with them. In his new understanding of history he put aside the concept of the enemy and brought all persons to the common table, where, of course, there can be no enemies. He talks of the fulfillment of the Kingdom by claiming that if one accepts his teachings, "I will sup with him." He does not attempt to explain some new order and new understanding of the law. To sup with the Messiah is certainly an obvious enough event.

In John's Gospel (my favorite), John claims that Jesus explains that anyone who eats and drinks with him, "abides in me and I in him." John has a wonderful way of talking of this eating. He uses words that we would apply to a dog gnawing upon a bone, not just eating; he used terms like "devour," "chew," or "gnaw" (John 6:54–58). When you offer a dog a bone, he does not sit there with his paws gently extended, as you and I do at the Eucharist. No, the dog jumps upon the offering and begins to gobble it up with gusto! That is how John claims we are to approach the feast.

Again, Jesus uses terms that a shepherd would understand when speaking of the care and protection of his flock. "Feed my sheep" refers to the pastor's responsibility to be faithful in his care of the members of his or her parish. The term "pastor" comes from "pasture;" the place for feeding.

I find it very amusing that Jesus should talk of us as sheep, but then he spoke to a herd-keeping people. Why do I find this reference to us as sheep amusing? Because sheep are one of the dumbest animals that we know, probably second in stupidity only to the turkey. Are we that stupid? The Bible seems to think so. Secondly, we are totally communal; without one another we will die. The same is true of sheep.

The Parables of the Table

The stories or parables that Jesus told very often centered around food and eating with the enemy.

We are quite sure that the parables represent the most authentic words of Jesus to be found in the Bible, and certainly his method of teaching through the parables is his and his alone. The stories that he told are offered for the sake of insight and vision, not for the sake of carefully stated factual information. One has to make some serious decisions about what the story could possibly mean. I suppose this method of teaching could be called the "Hot Potato Method" since Jesus seems to always throw a tough question to a listener who answers and tosses it back. Jesus then asks another question and the toss is on again. A perfect example is the Parable of the Good Samaritan.

A lawyer asks Jesus what he thinks is the most important part of the law in terms of the lawyer's own salvation. Jesus asks the lawyer what he thinks and the lawyer decides that one is to love God and love his neighbor as he does himself. Jesus replies that the lawyer has offered a good answer and leaves it at that. "But the lawyer, desiring to justify himself, says, 'But who is my neighbor?'" No room for error here as the lawyer wants clear and unmistakable information. Jesus then tells the story of the Good Samaritan which leaves the lawyer in a terrible legal bind.

According to the story, a man was traveling along a road between two cities and thieves fell upon him and beat him, robbed him, and left him on the side of the road to die. Several members of the clergy, good people who delighted in obeying the law, came upon him and passed by on the other side of the road. The bishop didn't stop to help, the local priest did not stop, nor did any other good person who came by. Why? Because it was very likely that this guy by the side of the road had been involved in some criminal activity himself, and was therefore unclean. The clergy could not afford to become involved since they would be defiled by this man's possible uncleanness and thus be worthless in terms of their responsibilities to the Temple. This was a very serious issue in those days, and we must not assume that the clergy were doing the wrong thing. In terms of the law they were doing the right thing.

Then a Samaritan came by and found the beaten man. Here is the hot potato, the clincher, the point of the story. Samaritans were so low on the social ladder that a good Jew would never be seen in the presence of such a character. Samaritans were considered religious heretics and outsiders. Therefore, at least in terms of the law, the Samaritan had nothing to lose. He was already in the pits, so he took the beaten man to an innkeeper, bound up the hurt man's wounds, and told the innkeeper that he would return in a few days when the poor fellow was better, and pay the bills for his keep.

Jesus then asks this astonishing question: "Who was a neighbor to this beaten man?" Had he asked the lawyer, "Who obeyed the law?" the lawyer would have to have answered, "All of those who passed by." But the poor lawyer was stuck. The question was about the neighbor, and Jesus turned the whole story around so that the lawyer had to say, "Well, the illegal outsider who should not have even cared, he was the neighbor who helped and fed the beaten one." What a thing to have to admit! Some days I feel sorry for the nitpicking lawyer, but he is better off now due to his new insight.

The Parable of the Prodigal Son is another that draws much attention in the Church in our time. However, there is a major point made in this parable that most of us miss, and it concerns a feast, of course.

The term "Prodigal" refers to one who is lavish and wastefully extravagant. The title fits this son perfectly. One day he demanded his share of his father's wealth and he took off and squandered his inheritance on harlots, loose living, and gambling. Finally he is broke and winds up feeding swine, not an appropriate occupation for a Hebrew. While he was starving he came to his senses and decided to return home and ask his father to let him live on the home land as a servant since he would then at least have food to eat.

Most of us know the rest of the story. As he approaches the house the father sees him coming and just goes through the roof with joy. The son begins to apologize and beg for forgiveness when the father shouts, "Bring quickly the best robe, and put it on him; and put a ring on his hand, and shoes on his feet; and bring the fatted calf and kill it, and let us eat and make merry; for this my son was dead, and is alive again; he was lost, and is found" (Luke 15:11–24). And the feast began.

The parable certainly points to the fact that God the Father is awaiting our return, but there is one item here that fascinates me. It was not the custom to have meat regularly in Biblical times as meat was eaten only on High Holy Days. What was this father doing with a fatted calf when there was no holiday in sight? In ancient Israel it was impossible to offer thanksgiving without a feast, and so this expectant old man, always waiting for God to pull off some wonderful thing, kept a fatted calf ready, just in case, just in case a thanksgiving feast should be necessary! I love this whole concept of each of us, you and me, being prepared with a fatted calf as we expectantly wait upon coming grand events, most unknown. Of course I do not mean something cheap for the feast like a pack of Twinkies and a six-pack of beer. I mean that we have a feast in the freezer, ready to go at a moment's notice, just like the old father kept a fatted calf in the yard. We never know when the Holy One will act!

Another parable, that of the Marriage Feast, again points to the fact that we should always be ready for a great event, ready at all times. Jesus told the story of a ruler who sent out invitations to his son's wedding feast. Now, you have to understand that one did not turn down an invitation to such a family feast during Jesus' time. Yet when everything was cooked, important guests called in with cheap excuses and the ruler was furious. He called his servants and sent them out into the streets to invite anyone who would like to come, both "bad and good" guests, and the hall was packed. It must have been a grand scene. However, when the ruler entered the hall he found a guest who was not dressed in a wedding garment. How could he have been, as he had just come in off the streets? The poor man was speechless. The host threw him out on the street. Jesus closes the story with this line: "For many are called but few are chosen" (Matthew 22:1–14). I know that this sounds terribly unreasonable but you certainly get the point. We are always to be ready for the feast, no matter what we are doing!

Eating with the Enemy

Many more stories were told by Jesus as he pointed to the new order of things. But he did some things that must have been considered quite odd, if not downright illegal. He stopped at Jacob's well for a drink and he had nothing with which to draw the water. A woman from Samaria approached the well and Jesus asked her for a drink. Now, we must understand that Jews were to have nothing to do with Samaritans as they were considered outside the faith. Not only that, but Jesus knew that this woman had had several husbands and she was not even married to the fellow that she was currently living with. More reasons to stay away from her. She would have been listed as an enemy. And Jesus asks her for a drink. Amazing!

Jesus was seen in public with another woman who would have caused a great bit of gossip: Mary Magdalene. Mary Magdalene had been possessed with seven demons and Jesus and Mary obviously shared meals together. This was risky business and Jesus used these events to point to his new understanding of history.

One more story, that of Zaccheus. My Sunday School teacher never did figure out the meaning of this wee little man and I did not understand him myself until I was in theological school. You see, Zaccheus was of our family in those days. He was your wife's brother-in-law's cousin. He was of us, but certainly not with us. In those days some Jews turned to collecting taxes for the Roman Empire, taxes that came from our pockets and were used to pay the Roman troops that held us in bondage. Zaccheus was a thoroughgoing traitor, and he was the enemy. Everybody hated him! Everybody we knew would not get near the guy. He would stop by your house every third Tuesday, holding his clipboard and his little calculator, and he would stand on the porch and compute your tax. Then, the upstart would add 15 percent more, which he would keep for himself. He called it "overhead." Oh, everyone hated him. He was a serious enemy.

We do not know how Jesus knew Zaccheus but he did. One day when the preacher from Nazareth was speaking, little Zaccheus tried to get into the circle so that he might see this man, this Jesus. Everybody hit Zaccheus on the shoulder or pushed him about so he climbed up into a tree in order to see what was going on. Right in the middle of a sermon, and right in front of everybody in town—that is to say, all of the nice folk—Jesus called up into the tree and told Zaccheus that he was to go home and prepare lunch. Jesus would be by in a few minutes to eat. Good Heavens, Jesus is going to eat with Zaccheus? You were not to eat with the enemy, and I cannot imagine the shock that these listeners must have felt. A new understanding of history and theology and the Law was unfolding right in front of them, and all at table!

This understanding of history showed a new and wonderful intention of the Law, a new understanding of the Law. In order to make this new inclusiveness known, this acceptance of the fact that *we must accept our enemies,* Jesus ate with them, and not just as an example. He actually ate with them!

Jesus ate with Zaccheus the tax collector, the Samaritan woman, Mary Magdalene, and he even invited one of the thieves who was crucified with him to feast with him in Paradise. The woman at the well should have been enough, but then we see the event at the meal in the Upper Room just before Jesus' death.

Judas, who I believe was a member of the guerrilla hill-fighting group that was trying to rid Palestine of the Roman invaders, sold the Man from Nazareth to the Romans. I really think that Judas expected Jesus to call forth some sort of cataclysmic event that would throw the routers out, but the result was the Crucifixion. Please note that Leonardo da Vinci did his homework well in terms of the text since in his painting of the Last Supper Judas is saying, "Someone is going to betray you? Is it I, Lord, is it I?" Jesus seems to have already expected the events that were about to take place and yet in the painting he is feeding Judas bread as poor Judas asks that abominable question. Lord, you are not to feed the enemy at your table. But Jesus did. He always did.

Biblical scholars have been trying to describe this man Jesus for centuries. We know little of what he did, but we know a great deal about what the early Church claimed about his presence. And we do know this for sure: *He ate with all of the wrong people!*

It is perfectly understandable, then, that all of the Resurrection appearances occurred at meals, all of them except that one at the tomb. The appearance in the Upper Room at another meal, the Road to Emmaus, the claim that he was the Bread and Wine of Life, and certainly the great fish fry.

This is a favorite appearance of mine. Simon Peter had gone back to fishing, along with several of the other disciples, depressed that his leader had been killed. They caught nothing that night and in the morning Jesus was standing on the beach. He told them where to fish and then Jesus set about to cook the fish himself. And they ate together. I think this is a very obvious commentary by the author, John, on the fact that Jesus was fully human as well as fully divine following the Resurrection. An early heresy in the Church, Docetism, claimed that Jesus was not fully human but only a spiritual appearance that looked like he was human. No, John refuted that heresy as he claimed that Jesus ate fish on the beach the day after the Resurrection. How could someone who was not human be bothered with fish for breakfast? Jesus was bothered by every need that we have, including our breakfast. He was hungry, too.

The line "And he was known to them in the breaking of the bread" (Luke 24:35) clearly points to the birth of the early Church. Jesus is suddenly seen as the companion, a word that stems from the Latin *com* (with) and *panis* (bread). In the breaking of the bread we know who and whose we are. The Church continues to make that claim to this day.

New Testament Worship and the Meal

We are quite sure that Jesus was familiar with, or perhaps even a part of, the Essene community. This early Jewish community had a long tradition of seeing the table as the place for serious celebration, and certainly the place for the coming of the expected Messiah. Each meal was offered in expectation of the coming of the Messiah, and out of this tradition, it seems to me, came the Eucharist.

Jesus was not the first one to bless bread and wine at a special meal. Surely he took on this tradition from the Essene community of his time and certainly the Jewish customs of his day.

However, when Jesus blessed the bread and the wine at the meal in the Upper Room, he claimed that the bread was his body offered to God and the wine was his blood offered as a symbol of a new covenant.

Wine becomes blood? What could this possibly mean?

Shepherds have always known about the blood of adoption. I had to learn about it from a shepherd as we rarely talked of such a thing in theological school. For Americans blood is messy and to be avoided, but not so with a shepherd.

Here is the background of the image of the blood of adoption. In the morning a shepherd awakes to find that a ewe has given birth to a child . . . and the child has died. In another portion of his flock the shepherd finds another ewe that gave birth during the night and the mother died! So, the shepherd has a childless mother on the one hand, and the mother will probably die of a broken heart. On the other hand he has an orphan. All logic tells him to put the orphan with the childless mother. Should work, shouldn't it? It will not work, not at all, as the mother knows the child is not hers and the child himself is confused and starving.

The old prophets and the old shepherds saw in this regular event in their flock a perfect image of our relationship to God. We are so alienated from one another that we are dying from starvation and God is dying of a broken heart. But one thing can be done, and only one. If the shepherd slits the throat of the dead lamb and drains his blood, he can then wash the orphan in the blood of the lamb, and the mother, smelling her own, immediately moves so that the orphan may suckle. In other words, the orphan is brought to table and to life by his adoption through the blood. The early Scriptures promised that a Messiah would come and be the lamb by which we were brought to an intimate relationship with God. The book of Revelation points to Jesus and joyfully proclaims: "Worthy is the Lamb who was slain, to receive power and wealth and wisdom and might and honor and glory and blessing!" (Revelation 5:12) And by His blood, the blood of adoption, we participate in these gifts. In short, we are brought home to feast, to the only meal that really matters. After all, the Bible sees us as outsiders in this world and we must be invited to the feast, and invited we are. By His blood we belong!

Further, when Jesus blesses the cup and the bread he urges us do the same often and promises that whenever we do this there he will be also. He never says, "Do this in remembrance of me," a phrase that is carved into thousands of Protestant altar tables. We use that term to connote only cerebral activity, an intellectual memory. In Greek the phrase is "Anamnesis," which I think is better translated "that I may be present!" The Eucharist is not something that we do in order to remember something, though that happens too, but we celebrate the meal that "He may be truly present," and at table with us. I no longer bother with the argument over whether or not the bread and wine become the physical and actual body and blood of Christ, since I have no problem in accepting the factual reality of His Presence. The bread and wine feed me, the body and blood give me life. All at table.

In very early services in the Church the anticipation of the coming of this presence at Eucharist was so high that people shouted, "Maranatha, the Lord comes!" I am personally terribly saddened at the lack of expectation in our contemporary services. I want to see the chalice raised with a bit of fright, serious fright, and I want to see the priest tremble when he or she says, "Behold, the Blood of the Lamb of God that takes away the sins of the world." The wine becomes the blood of adoption and we are brought home to the table . . . and we just sit there assuming the old Protestant slouch. Stand up and cheer, people, we have been invited to the Feast again!

One of the most beautiful services of the early Church is that of Saint Hippolytus. Since we all may have been hardened due to some of the chill brought about by the current trend toward informality in worship, I offer this beautiful liturgy that combines the Eucharist with a form of the love feast, a communal meal that was shared in very early Christian times. Not only are wine and bread blessed and offered but also oil, cheese and olives, milk and honey, and water. When I was a college chaplain my students delighted in this service as the bread and wine came with a complete breakfast! It might be fun for you to celebrate in this way some morning in your own parish.

Incidentally, a person in the early Church was ordained to collect money for the widows and orphans and clean up after the love feasts. He was called a "deacon." I still often wear my clerical collar along with my apron when I conduct the following service.

Saint Hippolytus was a theologian in Rome around A.D. 185.

THE CELEBRATION OF THE BODY OF CHRIST
ADAPTED FROM THE TRADITION OF
SAINT HIPPOLYTUS

Rome: ca. 200

THE GREETING   Peace be with you.
And with your spirit.

THE PSALM

OLD TESTAMENT LESSON

THE GOSPEL

THE SERMON

THE PRAYER OF THE FAITHFUL (adapted from the Church at Alexandria)

Deacon   (all standing) Pray for the peace of the one holy catholic and apostolic orthodox Church of God.

Silence   (all standing)

Presider   (all standing) We pray and ask your goodness, Lover of mankind: Remember, Lord, the peace of your one holy catholic and apostolic Church which is from one end of the world to the other: Bless all the peoples and all the lands: The peace that is from heaven grant in all our hearts, but also graciously give us the peace of this life.

We pray and ask your goodness, Lover of mankind: Remember, Lord, our leaders. Preserve them to us in safety many years in peaceful times, fulfilling those holy offices which you have committed to them according to your holy and blessed will, rightly dividing the word of truth, feeding your people in holiness and righteousness: And with them all the fullness of your one only holy catholic and apostolic Church.

Pray for this holy assembly and our meetings.

We pray and ask your goodness, Lover of mankind: Remember, Lord, our congregations. Grant that we may hold them without hindrance, that they may be held without impediment, according to your holy and blessed will: Through the grace of your only Son, Jesus Christ, our Lord, Amen.

KISS OF PEACE   (a sign of reconciliation)
Peace be with you.
And with your spirit.

THE OFFERTORY HYMN

THE THANKS   The Lord be with you.
And with your spirit.
Lift up your hearts.
We lift them up to the Lord.
Let us give thanks to the Lord.
It is fitting and right.

Presider   We return thanks to you, God, through your beloved Son, Jesus Christ, whom you sent to us, in these last days, as Savior, Redeemer, and Messenger of your will. He is your Word, inseparable from you. Through him you made all things. Being well pleased with him, you sent him from heaven into the womb of a virgin. Dwelling there, he was made flesh and was revealed as your Son, born of the Holy Spirit and the Virgin.

He, fulfilling your will and winning a holy people for you, stretched out his hands when he suffered that he might set free from suffering those who trusted in you.

Therefore, remembering his death and resurrection, we offer to you this bread and cup, giving you thanks that you have considered us worthy to stand in your presence and to serve you.

And we ask that you send your Holy Spirit on the offering of the holy Church. Unite all who share in these holy mysteries that they may be filled with the Holy Spirit for the strengthening of their faith in the truth, so that we may praise and glorify you through your Son Jesus Christ.

Through whom glory and honor be to you with the Holy Spirit in your holy Church both now and always. Amen.

THE BLESSING OF OIL

O God who sanctifies this oil, as You do grant unto all who are anointed and receive of it, hallowing wherewith You did kings and priests and prophets, so grant that it may give strength to all that taste of it and health to all that use it.

THE BLESSING OF CHEESE AND OLIVES

Lover of mankind, sanctify this solidified milk, solidifying us also unto Your good charity.

Grant also that this fruit of the olive depart not from Your sweetness, this fruit which is the type of Your fatness which You have caused to flow from the Tree for the life of them that hope in You.

THE BLESSING OF MILK AND HONEY

And bless this milk and honey mingled together in fulfillment of the promise which was made to the Fathers, wherein He said I will give you a land flowing with milk and honey; which Christ indeed gave, even His Flesh, whereby they who believe are nourished like little children, making the bitterness of the human heart sweet by the sweetness of His word.

THE BLESSING OF WATER

Bless this water also, for an oblation for a sign of the laver, that the inner man also, which is psychic, may receive the same rites as the body.

COMMUNION   (all gathering about the common table)
                     The bread of heaven in Christ Jesus.
                     Amen.
                     In the Holy Spirit and holy Church.
                     Amen.

PRAYER AND BENEDICTION (late additions from the Church in Ethiopia)

God Almighty, the Father of our Lord Jesus Christ, we give you thanks because you have imparted to us the reception of the holy mystery. Let it not be for guilt or condemnation, but for the renewal of soul and body and spirit, through your only Son through whom to you be all honor and glory world without end. Amen.

Everything is easy to prepare for this service. The bread and wine you know. Water is simply that. Milk and honey are blended by whipping a cup of honey into each quart of milk. This can be served in small glasses. For the cheese I have always used Greek feta along with Greek olives. The olive oil is blessed and a member of the congregation can go about, placing just a fingerprint of the oil on each person's forehead so that "our faces may shine."

Please remind your friends that it is all right to yell "Thank you" when served the bread and wine, or to yell "Amen," instead of those little quiet mumbles that we offer in church.

And remember that we are to jump upon the offered bread instead of just plunking it into our mouths and then pretending that we are not going to chew it.

The feasting on the bread and wine in the early Church always pointed to the future. Everything in the New Testament does! Further, since all feasts deal with some memory of the past, it is easy to see why all of the High Holy Days of the Church are called feasts. More about that later.

A Second Quick Summary

The New Testament traditions show Jesus as one who was familiar with the concept of food talk as God talk, and he used it often. His parables pointed to the table often and he used feasting as an image of the coming Kingdom. He ate regularly with those who were seen as enemies, thus pointing to a new understanding of the Law and history.

All of the Resurrection appearances took place at meals except the one at the tomb. "And he was known to them in the breaking of the bread." The Church still claims that this is how we "know" him.

American Table Images

Colonial Nomads All

We Americans share a bit of nomadism with those early Biblical people. After all, when the European discovered America he really was traveling as a nomad. He gave up his previous land in England and Europe (well, I suppose he had to!) and traveled to this country. Like nomads these immigrants had to share with each other during the ship's passage in order to make it to the New World alive. A family of five had a small trunk for their few allowable belongings, and one person in five was to die during the trip. (Why do we not discuss this in our history books? I suppose it is because the expected loss of life during the trip was taken as a given.)

When the Europeans reached these shores they were met by the Native Americans, the American Indians, who were nomads as well, moving about with the herds and living off the land. As with the Biblical nomadic traditions, the American Indians participated in the nomadic mind-set of sharing all things, even food with strangers.

So the Native American greeted us European strangers on these shores and taught us how to survive in the New World. He offered us corn and shared with us his growing methods. "One dead fish in the ground and two kernels of corn around it." That should really be our national motto, not "In God We Trust." We do not. It was the shared corn that kept us alive and the kindness of the American Indian, who has always shared everything communally, that got us through those first few winters.

Lord, is the Native American sorry now that he was so good to us.

In Colonial America communal sharing was the method, and food was passed about to those who needed it. Even the corn was owned by the community, not the individual. "Scraping the bottom of the barrel" refers to the salt-pork barrel, and when a mother ran out of salt pork she had to go to the neighbors.

As a child of the Pacific Northwest I see some similarities between the habits of the East Coast Natives and the Native Americans of our part of the country. The Kwakiutl Indians used to have a feast called a potlatch, in which the wealthy members of the tribe gave away their wealth in order to show how wealthy they really were. Get it? It was sort of an outdoing of one another in gift giving. The potlatch is the main way in which the status of a person could be changed within the tribe.

My wife, Patty, who has the mind of an anthropologist, claims that the nomadic ethic so common among Indian tribes is probably the reason why they have so much trouble in understanding the private Protestant Work Ethic. The American work ethic claims that you must hoard your wealth so that you can separate yourself and your family from the largest number of persons possible. The Nomadic Ethic claims that everything is to be shared.

We have a friend who is a member of the Yakima tribe and who, quite by accident, came into a sizable inheritance. Since he had been raised by his grandma, he knew the old ways . . . thus he paid off all of his relatives' bills, leaving little for himself. With the remains of his inheritance he threw a party for his friends. So it goes with nomads!

How did we move from a Colonial Nomadic Ethic to an Ethic of Privatude in our time? It has something to do with the movement away from the great communal feasts that George Washington and Thomas Jefferson threw to the private eating of the likes of Diamond Jim Brady, who ate most of his enormous meals privately. This movement marked the rise of the American dream.

Rise of the American Dream

A cuisine is a way of thinking more than it is a way of eating. When we want to get to know a culture well it seems to me we should study its eating habits first, and then study its history, art, and philosophy.

When we begin to study the changes in American eating habits we cannot help but see the movement from the communal life-style common in Colonial times to the value of privacy in our time. Individualism and privatism are based on the ability to get along on one's own. The old freedom of choice rule means infinite variety and absolute independence. Our eating habits point to these values. We seem to be eating more and more by ourselves. Much of our food is sold with that very habit in mind. Certainly Snack Packs and junk food packaged for one person are strictly private matters. And the table? How can a family communicate if they are all eating their dinner while sitting in a car staring straight ahead?

In our long quest for the American dream—that is, our ability to get along without anyone else, the pull-yourself-up-by-your-own-bootstraps trip—we have moved from communal thinking to private thinking. Perhaps we have reached our supposed goal? We don't even have to cook food for ourselves anymore, let alone for anyone else. The salad bar at the super-market symbolizes for me the desire of so many to work themselves to death and then go home and eat alone, with little communication with family or friends. We are just too busy for such things! Well, if this has been our goal, and I am convinced that it has been, then we have made a very profound discovery during the trip from communal thinking to private thinking. We have discovered that the only real gift of privatude is loneliness. And it hurts! We have older people who live by themselves, absolutely alone. They are our parents and we claim that we are so very proud of them. "She does so well living all by herself." She is probably dying of loneliness, but then, she is so strong.

Private eating has given rise to a very popular artistic sym-bol in our time. What symbolizes the call to privatude, indepen-dence, freedom of choice, variety, better than the Swanson TV dinner? It is perfect. It marks the collapse of communal family eating and thinking and eventually the collapse of our culture. I mean this! Mrs. Swanson is of the Antichrist! Such a loss, our family table.

The invention of the TV dinner was expected in our time. Following World War II few woman wanted to return to the daily task of meal preparation, and men certainly were not going to do it. So, during the early fifties came the first frozen chicken pot pie and then the TV dinner. It was no longer necessary for families to eat together and the evening dinner began to pass away. Am I claiming that what we used to call the Generation Gap was due to the TV tray? I am coming close to that.

I was a college chaplain during the sixties and students were much more interested in living in a commune than they were in living in a marriage. It took me a while to figure it out but I came to this: The college students of the sixties had all been raised in homes that celebrated this new privatude, this freedom of choice in the TV dinner. "Sorry I can't be home for dinner. Got basket-ball practice!" Dining at home with the family didn't much matter. In the evenings we all heated up a different TV dinner—freedom of choice, you know—and then sat in front of the television eating off those funny TV trays, the ones that shook and wiggled with every bite. And we watched *Gunsmoke*. No one spoke to anyone in the family, and if someone did speak while Doc on *Gunsmoke* was speaking, we shot him! And we did all of this in what we called The Family Room.

It is no wonder that students would come to me and tell me that they were moving in with one another, but they had no intention of getting married. Their family life had been so uncommunicative that they wanted nothing to do with a marriage license. So, off to a commune where they talked to one another constantly and where the evening meal was always declared to be a feast for this reason or for that.

Years later I married a lot of those kids . . . and they went off to have children and build houses. But you know, they did not build family rooms. They built dining rooms and are eating together! Surely there is hope for us.

Fast Foods/Prepared Foods and Creativity

Let me tell you why I am hopeful.

We now have a whole generation of kids who have grown up not knowing a thing about a real waffle, a real milk shake, or a good batch of homemade mashed potatoes with real gravy. They have been raised on prepared foods since neither parent had the time to cook. For the working parent prepared foods were not only an out, they were a blessing. Cooking was just not a necessity.

Marshall McLuhan, media guru of the sixties, claimed that whenever something ceased to be a necessity it could become an art form. He cited the movies as an example. For generations movies were our main source of information. Remember the crowing rooster and the weekly news? But when television came along, offering greater immediacy and access to news, the movies lost their function of news gathering and turned instead to making motion pictures as a serious art form. Everyone claimed that television would be the death of the movies but it wasn't. McLuhan was right. When something ceases to be a necessity it can become an art form.

Surely we must apply this observation to cooking in our time. No one has to cook anymore as you can live out of the pre-pared food aisles without any difficulty whatsoever. In McLuhan terms, this could mean new hope for real cooking and family communication in our times.

Years ago a dear friend, Sara Little Turnbull, claimed that by the year 2000 home cooking would be an art form. "Oh, I could never paint. But I do cook!" "Well, I could never do that!" The funny thing is that it has already happened. Prepared and fast foods have given us the time and freedom to see cooking as an art form, a form of creative expression. No, I am not saying that people who see cooking as an art form cook every night. They do not. But more and more people are spending two or three nights a week in the midst of a serious encounter with their kitchen, and thus with the dining-room table. In an odd way, prepared foods have allowed us the time to cook from scratch.

This cooking as art form could very well give us a new form of feasting, of celebrating with one another. The words "Come on over. I'm cooking!" will mean something more than it has ever meant.

American Table Manners
and the Puritan Ethic

The Puritan Ethic has really caused havoc at the American dinner table, as it has encouraged the rejection of our basic passions. The insights of Aristotle and Socrates, which valued reason over the passions, have resulted in a very calculated way of doing and seeing things in this land of ours.

The focus on rationalism by these philosophers and the Puritans obliged us to reject our emotions as being inferior to practical insight. Since hunger is one of the most basic passions, and it is very real, we began to see a rational and not a celebrative approach to the table. American table manners stem from this rejection.

Our need for control over our passions has resulted in a dinner party that never really takes place. Oh, we eat all right, but it is hardly a party. Certain rules, called table manners, point to the fact that we must not delight in the meal since we don't need it anyhow. The host or hostess announces dinner and we are to stay in the living room sipping sherry until the announcement is made a second time. God forbid we should run to the table and confess our hunger by acting as if we were truly ready to eat. Instead we are to stand about until the third call when the cook pleads with us "to come now or the salmon will be ruined." At that point it is all right to walk slowly to the table. We are in charge of our emotions here.

During the meal our table manners dictate that we must deny that we are eating. One hand in the lap, the dumbest place in the world for one hand! Our Canadian neighbors have enough sense to use two eating implements at once. Our effort to claim that we can get along very well without food, or for that matter the kindness of our hosts, means that we must refuse second helpings unless our arm is truly twisted. How rude it would be to confess our hunger for good company and good food and good wine and blurt out, "I thought you would never ask if I wanted more. This is just great and I thank you for it!"

I do not believe that our culture is too materialistic. If we accept Creation as a gift of God, then we are not materialistic enough! That is to say, we should be cheering at each meal, anticipating each dinner party, carefully examining each wine bottle, so that, in the end, each meal is seen as a celebration of the fact that God has given us this world along with all of its treasure stores of mushrooms and artichokes and asparagus and pork ribs and lightly smoked salmon. Puritans have trouble dancing at such a feast and I think it is a shame. A damn shame!

The Future of
the Feast

Can We Last Without the Feast?

We as a culture rarely feast since we have moved away from corporate eating to private eating. We do recognize the feast of Thanksgiving and the Fourth of July, not our best eating day. The rest of our holidays are connected with our religious commitments. We have few cultural feasts in our time.

What is a culture? Webster's definition is helpful here. "Culture is the integrated pattern of human knowledge, belief, and behavior that depends upon man's capacity for learning and transmitting knowledge to succeeding generations." A culture, as I see it, is based upon a group of people held together by common memories. Language or race or ethnicity are not really the issues, our own nation being a perfect example of a common memory being shared by many persons of diverse racial and ethnic backgrounds.

In his *Christianity and Culture*, T. S. Eliot offers this insight: "If we take culture seriously, we see that a people does not need merely enough to eat (though even that is more than we seem able to ensure) but a proper and particular cuisine: one symptom of the decline of culture in Britain is indifference to the art of preparing food. Culture may even be described simply as that which makes life worth living. And it is what justifies other peoples and other generations in saying, when they contemplate what remains and the influence of an extinct civilisation, that it was worth while for that civilisation to have existed."

Cooking and eating may not be simply a means of existing, but feasting is one of the things that makes existing at all worthwhile.

THE MEMORY OF FEASTING

Feasting is also closely related to memory. We eat certain things in a particular way in order to remember who we are. Why else would you eat grits in Madison, New Jersey? I am Norwegian by blood and every Christmas Eve we feast on lutefisk. I hate lutefisk but on Christmas Eve I must remember who I am, and my background.

We pass the memories of our past history on to our children through the feast, the memorable meal. Feasting is the very best way we have of helping the next generation understand their own heritage. For those of us who were born during World War II, a time of sugar ration stamps and little meat, a sugar feast might be in order. For those grandchildren who heard stories of their grandma keeping the family alive with little other than cornmeal, a fried cornmeal mush feast is called for. That was my grandma. For those who fled China during difficult times, the New Year's Feast becomes a method of keeping generations attached to one another through the images of certain foods and the memories they bring forth.

Consider your own childhood. Think of the very best times that you shared with your family and I am sure that the dining-room table will come to mind. Remember the smell of the kitchen. Close your eyes and smell those aromas, those memories. The brain remembers odors and smells and scents better than just about anything else. Lin Yutang, the great philosopher, put it this way: "What is patriotism except the memories of the good things that we ate as a child?"

Where am I going with all of this? It is simple. If by culture we mean those common memories that hold a group of people together, and if we see that feasting and memory are directly related, then the best way to pass on our culture is through the meal, the feast.

If a culture ceases to feast, and ours nearly has, will it cease to be a culture? I think so. As a matter of fact, I am terrified that we may lose our young to the fast-food game. *It is very obvious that TV dinners have no memories!* None whatsoever! How does it feel to know that someday your grandson may very well ask your great-grandson, "Do you want to know what your great-grandmother used to defrost for us?" You see, it does not work. Nothing will be remembered in terms of the family history, in terms of the culture, in terms of the appreciation of a people-hood.

Incarnational Theology and the Table

How far should we go with the feasting? Genesis claims that when God created the earth He/She looked at it and declared it to be good. Very good indeed, especially the foods. The Psalms and Second Isaiah urge us to "delight ourselves in fatness," here referring to that beautiful image of fulfillment and joy, a hope among a people that spent most of their time starving.

I think we are starving in our time, though we have ample food to eat. It is simply not fulfilling unless it is shared at a feast. We are hungry for meaning much more than for food.

The doctrine of the Incarnation, the belief that God has declared His/Her Serious Presence in this place, this earth, under the current confines of history, means that the beautiful claim of Genesis is confirmed. God loves this place, and everything in it. The Cross as a symbol of this Serious Presence in the world gives us permission to enjoy Creation. No holds barred. What a joy!

"How can you, Jeff Smith, a clergyman, derive so much joy from the table when there are people who are hungry?" I have to answer this question since I know you are going to ask it. Someone always does. It is a very profound question.

I am not capable of solving the international hunger problem as it is a matter involved in politics, and I am not a politician. However, as a Christian I am obligated to feed the hungry, and I do that. I do that in many ways that you will never hear about. But to say that you should stop enjoying the blessings of the table when others are hungry seems to me like saying that I am not to love my wife since there are so many who are lonely. It does not make sense. My job is to teach people how to enjoy the table and all that it means and to help, in some small way, to put something to eat on that table. I like to think that I do that.

Can you imagine Abraham, Moses, Second Isaiah, or Jeremiah sitting down at the Puritan table? No, they would be ready to enjoy, and the Puritan would be ready for discipline. What a bore!

Who are we to refuse God's cleverness? We are to be responsible with the world and Creation, but it is God's gift to us. I love Studs Terkel on Chicago radio, and I love his closing line each week. "Take it easy, but take it." That is how we are to see the feast.

The Seasonal Feast

In very early times great seasonal feasts were held. At the end of a good summer a feast was held as a thanksgiving. When the new spring arrived a feast of welcome was prepared. After all, the people had lived through the dead of winter and a party needed to be called forth. There were feasts of plenty and feasts of want, but in each case the feasts marked the history and passage of a people.

In our time seasonal feasts cease to be so important since we no longer know seasons in terms of our food sources. I can buy strawberries in January and artichokes and mushrooms all year-round. Since we no longer see seasonal food trends we cease to have seasonal feasts. This may turn out to be a great loss. I think it better to celebrate the strawberry at the height of the local berry growing season than to offer my family inferior berries from some other clime all of the year-round. They will never understand the flavor and the festival behind that grand season that I knew as a boy. Back then my mother would give me a little wooden box and take me out to a berry field. She would work and pick for us, as she always did, and then she would ask me what I had in my little box. "Three!" I could say . . . but my lips were very stained with the redness of that precious season.

I suppose that historically feasting was also a response to famine. A feast was held when we were about to embark upon a terrifying season, and a feast was held when we had somehow managed to live through a terrifying season. In our time we feel that we have solved the problem of technical famine and we now eat out of spiritual hunger and loneliness. I don't see much difference between that and plain old famine.

FASTING

A quick note on the concept of fasting. In a Puritanical world, or a Hellenistic world, Creation is seen as that which is holding captive the true nature of things. At death the true idea of things is set free to join some sort of universal ideal. I think that this implies the Creator made a mistake in Creation. One must then purge himself of desire for the tastes of the world in order to be "cleansed," thus pointing to a dirty, dirty world.

The image of a Sacramental Universe, one in which the Holy One created the world as a good place, filled with good things means that when one fasts he/she is doing it as an act of confession. How wonderful this Creation is, and how wonderful it tastes. One need fast for only a short time before one confesses that he/she is not God, but very happy to be dependent upon God's gorgeous Creation. Christians and Jews do not need to fast in order to get rid of the world, but rather in order to see who and whose they are.

American Consumption Ethic Versus the Biblical Ethic

I do not want you to think that in the midst of all this feasting talk I support the American Consumption Ethic. I do not. We consume far more than our share of the world's resources just to produce the abundance of food that we enjoy. Much of those resources are used in producing the fuel to create prepared and fast food items.

In the midst of every discussion on ecology in our time, someone always seems to be of the opinion that we consume so much because consumption is a Biblical admonition. Not so. In Genesis it does say, "Be fruitful and multiply, and fill the earth and subdue it; and have dominion over the fish of the sea and over the birds of the air and over every living thing that moves upon the earth" (Genesis 1:28). But with this gift of Creation came also the responsibility of keeping it in order. Adam and Eve were charged with that responsibility; they even had to name the animals. The idea that that line in Genesis gives us permission to raid the earth is absurd.

The source of overconsumption is not a Biblical idea but rather a very American one. Our move from communal living to privatude has been very costly, very costly indeed. It costs a lot of money to have so many people living the private life.

We cannot live this way much longer. The Bible claims that we are to share all things with one another. Don't pin American overconsumption on the Bible.

Feminism and the Biblical Table

In prehistoric times women were the gatherers. They brought to the table grains and seeds and roots and primitive vegetables. They gathered these with the use of wooden tools, tools that long ago have disintegrated. Men, on the other hand, were the hunters and they used tools chipped from stone, arrowheads and the like, tools that we still have. So we assumed that men controlled the food line and women simply backed it up with a few vegetables. While we now know that these are not the facts, it is true that women were given a place of lesser importance when it came to providing food for the family in early times.

The truth of the matter is that by Biblical times the women were cooking and baking constantly and they had time for little else. This has been true up until the last few generations in this country as well. Why was your grandmother not a great painter? Are you kidding? She had all she could do to keep the family alive. She cooked night and day, generally with little in terms of varieties of foods. We have not given women enough credit for keeping us all alive.

The Roman Church has been reluctant to ordain women as priests, claiming that the closest twelve followers of Jesus were all men. I find this to be an odd claim since there were very close female followers of Jesus present at every event in his ministry. Women were the first to come to the tomb at the time of the Resurrection. Women were crucial in the story of the Crucifixion. When Lazarus was raised from the dead it was his sisters, Mary and Martha, who discussed the event with Jesus. And dear Mary Magdalene, who appears in the Gospels on the same page as a harlot, was not one, of course. She was one of Jesus' dearest friends and if the Gospels are correct, then she talked with him at very crucial moments in his ministry. Should the Church find it odd that a woman probably heard the confessions of Jesus? Not at all!

The Church must also remember that according to the scriptures God chose a woman to be the vessel for the Son. Mary was more than a mother to Jesus. Not only did God choose to come through a woman but that very woman shapes the Gospels in her telling of the events of Jesus' life after he was taken from her. "And Mary pondered these things in her heart."

One of the dearest friends of my life is often referred to as the "mother of the feminist movement in theology." Her name was Nelle Morton and she explained to me one day that you could not translate the Hebrew names for God as being either masculine or feminine. God is androgynous, the best of both sexes. Since the New Testament was written by men, God is referred to only as male. In the English translation, even the term "children of God" is translated as "sons of God." Further, what do you do with such feminine and nurturing phrases as Jesus saying, "How often would I have gathered your children together as a hen gathers her brood under her wings . . . " (Matthew 23:37).

Does this sound like we are getting too far away from the Biblical table? Let me try one more. In John's Gospel a most beautiful and most often quoted line is offered. "For God so loved the world that He gave his only begotten Son . . . " (John 3:16). This is obviously a reference to the shepherd image of washing an orphan lamb in the blood of another dead lamb from a different mother. (See page 60 for a more complete discussion of this matter.) This is a wonderful image of adoption brought to grand theological heights, but God as "He"? It was the mother sheep that gives the son who becomes the image of adoption. The father sheep would not have been involved in such an event at all. He would be off looking for another ewe. In short, it is the feminine side of God that gives the Son, the motherly nurturing side of God that offers the sacrifice, not God as He but God as She.

In the Bible it is God as She who sets the table, invites us to the feast, and does the theological dishes!

The Future of the American Table

It is my belief that the best way to learn about another culture is at table. It is at table with another people that we really begin to understand what they are all about. Certainly the only way that we can claim to be a civilized culture is to be sensitive to the other cultures on this small planet. Understanding our table and eating habits will certainly help. No one wants to go to war against someone who can make a first-class borscht!

As a family we have always tried to teach our children about other cultures through food. I have fed my boys everything that you can imagine since I really did not want them to think any particular people to be weird. I have fed them jellyfish salad from China, oxtails in peanut sauce from the Philippines, octopus salad from Greece, headcheese salad from Rome, and on and on. I think my plan has worked out well and I offer the following story as evidence.

When Channing was in junior high school he was cool. He was cool! You remember how difficult it was to be cool in junior high. You had to hang out with the right people, and all of the right people were just as nervous as you were. I do not know how any of us even lived through that anxious period of our lives. Well, Channing was playing it cool one day, leaning against the wall in the main hallway, with his hands in his pockets, next to more cool guys. Suddenly, the guy next to him pointed and said, "There he is. The new kid from Poland. He even speaks with an accent!" Do you remember how tough it was to be on the outside? I was very proud to hear that Channing ran up to the kid and asked, "Are you really from Poland?" "Yes," was the reply. Channing inquired, "Hey, what's your favorite filling for pirogi?" Friends. Friends in a foreign land.

I am tired of the wars and battles based on some sort of assumed misunderstanding. *I believe that we will be able to call ourselves truly civilized only when we have more chefs than soldiers!*

Maybe we should put the chefs of the world in charge of the wars!

I can see it now. The battle is about to take place in a great banquet hall. There is an enormous cooking center in the middle of the hall, bleachers filled with spectators seated all around.

The battle begins: "I'll see your sauce and raise you an artichoke!"

"Ha! A Washington State Chardonnay to you!"

This is a war even the children could watch. The stove would get hot and the dishes would fly. An insult here and an insult there. A bit of laughter from our side over the terribly complicated dish that the French are trying to prepare. Then the Italians would enter. We would have to wait a couple of hours before they could begin to cook. They have to form a new government first!

And so it would go. Then, to the table and the sharing and the feasting.

No enemies here!

When the whole event was over we would gather up the leftovers just as in Saint John's Gospel at the feeding of the five thousand. There would be twelve baskets of leftovers, exactly.

Finally, the confessions at the table.

The Jews and the Arabs would demand a table together. The incredibly healing noise of their communal meal would cause all of the rest of us to look about as if we were embarrassed to be present at a party that we did not truly understand.

Do you remember that Associated Press photograph on the front page of the paper in 1977? It showed Menachem Begin, the prime minister of Israel, eating with Anwar Sadat, the president of Egypt. Enemies for thousands of years, two peoples who knew the rule about not eating with your enemies, are sharing a meal at a common table.

I could see some other characters at this great feast to heal the wounds of history.

George Wallace and Angela Davis would be sitting together eating grits, and loving it!

Saddam Hussein would lean over to Bill Clinton and say, "So, tell me. What do you think of Iraqi food?"

"Well, by golly, I didn't know that I liked Iraqi food. Look at all those dates. What do you think of our American pot roast?"

"Hmmmm," says Saddam. "I didn't think I would like it. You know, it's kind of sweet like the foods of the desert."

"Hey, I hadn't thought of that," replies Clinton. "We have to do this more often. Next time at my house. It's white! You have got to taste my Arkansas barbecue sauce!"

"I don't eat pork."

"Oh, yeah. I forgot."

The things we could learn about one another!

They shall hunger no more, neither
    Thirst any more;
  The sun shall not strike them, nor
    any scorching heat.
For the lamb in the midst of the
    Throne will be their shepherd,
  And he will guide them to springs
    Of living water;
And God will wipe away every tear
  From their eyes.

                        Revelation 7:16–17

Recipes from the Biblical Table

Diet in Biblical Times

When it came to diet, things were pretty tough for the average person in Biblical times. We hear so much these days about "the Mediterranean Diet," but we have to remember that many of the foods that make the Mediterranean Diet so attractive were just not available to the common person in Biblical lands two thousand years ago.

Ben Sirach offers a daily diet in his writings in the Apocrypha, the Book of Ecclesiasticus (39:26). Every day one ate pretty much the same thing. Bread, salt, milk and honey, olive oil, and, of course, wine. During a very good week you might have some dried fish or olives. Meat was eaten only on High Holy Days. The diet was bread, oil, and wine three times a day. Perhaps some cheese would show up now and then, but we must remember that such things were very scarce unless you were wealthy and of the ruling class.

These restrictions certainly did not apply to such wonderful characters as King Solomon, who could afford to order "ten fat oxen, and twenty pasture-fed cattle, a hundred sheep, besides harts, gazelles, roebucks, and fatted fowl" (I Kings 4:23). Sounds like he was having a few people in. For the rest of us we could not afford to kill off the animals that gave us milk and clothing, as well as helping work in the fields. That is all there was to it!

There were vegetables available, but they must have been costly. After all, the Promised Land turned out to be desert. The Children of Israel remembered the good foods from Egypt and had to settle for a very limited diet in their new home. The most common vegetables were probably leeks, onions, cucumbers, and, of course, garlic. With these, along with a few herbs and spices that only the wealthy could afford, one had to develop a sort of cuisine.

One can better understand the nature of the short-tempered Roman soldiers who were occupying Jerusalem during the first century. They had come from a fine culinary tradition that celebrated many grains and an endless variety of vegetables. They had been taught by the Greeks to make fabulous breads with seeds, herbs, and spices. They carried dried fruits with them when out conquering, another unwilling gift from the enslaved Greek chefs. Off the Romans went to take on Egypt, and while there, they ate very well. It was claimed that the soils of Egypt were so rich that all one had to do was to stick a seed in the mud and then come back a few months later for the harvest. The Romans indeed ate very well in Egypt.

The fax that came from Roman headquarters must have upset the troops right away since it directed them to conquer Palestine. Palestine? Where in the world is that? And, worse yet, when they arrived to take over, they found a people existing on a very limited diet. The Roman boys were unhappy, to say the least. I am sure that their hunger for foods from their own land was one of the things that caused them to be so nasty to the peoples of Jerusalem.

Can you not hear them yelling, "Even Egypt was better than this!"?

Foodstuffs Common
in the Biblical World

I have prepared a list of foodstuffs that would have been available in the ancient Holy Land. We must remember, however, that everything was seasonal and certainly not like our supermarkets with a year-round food supply.

Looking at this list, you will probably decide that the diet was not so restricted after all. But consider this: No one had all of these ingredients to cook with at any one time. Never! Everything was limited to a season, everything.

BIBLICAL FOODS

Please remember that while all of the following foods were available in ancient times, most of these items could only be afforded by the wealthy. The peasant diet was rather bland.

Vegetables and Legumes

Anise	Fennel	Onions
Artichokes	Leeks	Sorrel
Beans	Lentils	
Cucumbers	Mustard Greens	

Fruits

Apricots	Mulberries	Quinces ("Apples")
Dates	Muskmelon	Raisins
Figs	Olives	
Grapes	Pomegranates	

Spices

Anise	Cinnamon	Mustard
Black Caraway ("Fennel Flower")	Coriander	Saffron
	Cumin	
Caraway		

Herbs

Bay Leaves	Dill	Parsley
Capers	Garlic	Sage
Coriander	Hyssop	Thyme

Grains and Seeds

Barley	Emmer (Cheap Wheat)	Wheat (Spelt)
Bulgur (Parched Grain)	Millet	
Cracked Wheat	Sesame	

Nuts

Almonds	Pistachios	Walnuts

Meats

Cattle (Beef)	Fowl (Chicken)	Pigeons (Squab)
Fish (Fresh and Dried)	Lamb	Quail

Milk and Milk Products

Butter	Cheese Cakes	Yogurt
Cattle Milk	Sheep's Milk	

Miscellaneous

Honey	Vinegar	Wine

Recipes for Ancient Feasting

Many of the recipes in this book are as close to what I think went on in early times as we could possibly make them. Other recipes use these ancient ingredients in contemporary ways. You'll notice that there are no lettuce salads, no pasta dishes, no fancy sauces over lamb. For the most part, however, these are very healthy dishes, which are certainly compatible with our American diet. Use them to teach your kids about what went on in the land of the Bible two thousand years ago.

There are very few ingredients in these recipes that will be hard to find. Middle Eastern markets carry the odd things like pomegranate juice or molasses, as well as sumac and hyssop. Health food stores and food co-ops have the necessary grains and seeds. The rest of the items you should be able to find in a supermarket.

I think you will enjoy the breads. I know that you will enjoy the lamb cooked in grape leaves and the fish in leaves as well. We have included enough grain dishes to qualify for a farm subsidy. Some of these grains will be new to you, but worth seeking out.

The ingredients are discussed before each recipe, so I am confident that you and your family will pride yourselves on being able to cook delicious meals that would have charmed even the Roman troops.

A Guide to Unusual Ingredients

BLACK CARAWAY
("Fennel Flower")

This spice is great in breads. It can be found in Middle Eastern markets; it is not the same as regular caraway seed.

BULGUR WHEAT

This ingenious invention of the desert goes back to Biblical times. Grains of wheat were chopped up, then soaked in water until plump and set out on cloths in the sun to dry. The Bible calls it "parched grain"; we call it bulgur wheat. Today, wheat kernels are steamed, then dried and cracked. Bulgur can be purchased in any bulk grain store, food co-op, or Middle Eastern market, and in many supermarkets. It comes in three different grain sizes, fine, medium, and coarse, and can be baked, cooked in pilafs, or soaked and used in salads. Each recipe will tell you which size you need to use. I love this stuff.

CORIANDER
(Fresh and Seed)

Fresh coriander looks very much like parsley, but one whiff of this pungent herb will let you know it's coriander. It can be found in most supermarkets, or, try an Asian market (it's also called Chinese parsley) or a Mexican market. Coriander seeds can be purchased in any supermarket spice section.

CRACKED WHEAT

Often confused with bulgur, cracked wheat is not precooked, but just cleaned and cracked. Also available in fine, medium, or coarse textures, it can be found in grocery stores. Use in breads and grain dishes, though it takes much longer to cook than bulgur wheat does.

HYSSOP

A sweet herb that tastes like a cross between mint, licorice, and thyme. Fresh, it is great in salads, though you will probably have to grow your own in your herb garden. Call a good garden center for starter plants. When dried, it is often mixed with other herbs and spices of the Middle East. It can be purchased dried in a good spice shop or in a Middle Eastern market.

MULBERRIES

Hard to find these days, this berry tastes like a cross between a raspberry and a blackberry. If you wish to use fresh berries, you can certainly substitute a mixture of raspberries and blackberries. However, in these recipes we have used dried mulberries. They have a lovely sour flavor and can be found in any good Middle Eastern grocery. Dried cherries may also be substituted.

QUINCE

This is most likely what the English Bible refers to as the "apple." Apples are very American and were not around in Biblical times. So, Eve offered Adam a quince, a fruit that looks like a cross between an apple and a pear. It is yellow and smells of apple, pear, pineapple, and even banana. They appear in Asian and farmers' markets in the fall; use them in pies or to make jams. Allow them to ripen fully before using. Just leave them on the counter until they offer a rich and ripe aroma. Be sure to taste them before cooking with them, as some varieties are rather bitter.

SAFFRON

Saffron is the stigma of the crocus flower. Since it is hand-harvested and so much is required for a significant amount, it is the most expensive of all spices. It was used only by the very wealthy during Biblical times. Saffron is available as stigmas or powder; I prefer the former. The smaller the amount you buy, the more you will pay. I buy mine in one-ounce cans. It runs about sixty dollars per ounce in Seattle, but I buy top-quality saffron for around thirty dollars from Kalustyan's in New York. Remove it from its fancy, but not airtight, little tin and store it in a sealed canning jar in a dark, cool place. You need only a pinch to glorify your food. An ounce will last a long time.

SUMAC

Do not pick sumac from your backyard, but rather buy this wonderful spice in any Middle Eastern market. Our domestic sumac could make you ill, but the sumac from the Holy Land will delight you. Use it on breads, salads, over grains, and in soups and stews. I also use it on fried eggs.

TAHINI

A sort of sesame peanut butter that can be found in any Middle Eastern market and most fancy groceries. It is a very old food. It can be used in dressings, appetizers, soups, and desserts.

WHEAT

Go to the health food store and buy whole wheat berries. You can grind them, sprout them, or simmer them in broth. In Biblical times a cheaper form of what we know as wheat, called emmer, was used. Another form of ancient wheat was called spelt. Both can be found today, in most food co-ops and health food stores. I have tried all of these forms of wheat and have had the best luck with wheat berries.

ZA'ATAR

This herb and spice blend is made up of sesame seed, sumac, thyme, and, often, hyssop. You can buy it ready-made in any

Middle Eastern store. It is great on bread and goes well with many vegetables. Eggs and za'atar is a favorite breakfast dish at our home.

For the Vegetarian

Those of us who are not vegetarian are going to have to discipline our eating habits in the future, whether we like it or not. No, I am not going to do this by choice, but rather by necessity. The facts of the situation are too plain, as are the implications for our diet. In the very near future, depleted energy sources, exhausted land, scarce water, and enormous increases in population are going to combine to change the total structure of our diet.

We are going to have to reduce our dependency on red meat, since we will have fewer acres on which to raise the great American hamburger. Further, water shortages will affect our ability to raise cattle. Those cows are expensive! Our croplands are already stretched to the limit and that means that we cannot, given the expected increase in our population, provide more land for meat. The result is that we will be eating a much leaner diet, a diet that will be based on fewer meats and dairy products and more grains, potatoes, and beans. Even seafood will become scarce. In short, *The New York Times* predicts that by the year 2050, which is really just a few weeks away, we will be eating a diet that is close to that which was sustaining in Biblical times.

We depend a great deal upon oil to raise our cattle at the moment, and we know that the oil reserves are going to run out.

That is all there is to it! We are going to have to prepare for a diet that is lower in terms of red meat content, perhaps in terms of all meat, and learn to get along on a diet more akin to that of Biblical times. We have lived "high on the hog" for many generations, and now it seems time to change. No, I will not like it, but it is inevitable. Simply inevitable.

I am not so sure that this is going to be a bad time. Since the diet will contain more grains and fewer fats, it will certainly be much healthier for us. Further, it means that spareribs and sauerkraut will be relegated to a Sunday feast, for meat will be scarce. In the meantime, we will enjoy creative cooking using the ingredients that were available two thousand years ago. It is a strange turn of events, but we will make it, and I expect that we will enjoy it, or at least learn to enjoy it. I am optimistic, really I am. The following recipes will help you understand that.

My son Jason is a vegan, which, he explains, is a strict vegetarian eating only plants. Other vegetarians will eat plants and dairy products. The next stage down, or up, depending on your vision of things, is the eater who does not eat red meat, but eggs, chicken, fish; all of these are fine, but no mammals. Finally, there is what I am going to call the normal eater of the future, one who has cut down on red meat intake out of sheer financial necessity.

Thomas Jefferson would approve of such a diet. He rarely ate red meat, though he did serve a great deal of meat to his contemporaries. His real delight was to be found in vegetables, and he claimed that meat was to be used only for flavoring his beloved garden dishes, never as a main course. The Chinese have always thought this way, and we must learn to think this way as well.

Perhaps when this change of thought comes about, the argument between the vegetarians and the meat eaters will come to an end. I have been harassed by some of the most vicious people claiming that since I eat meat I must be nasty. I have been screamed at by people who claim that since they are strict vegetarians, they are more gracious than meat eaters. And, to tell you the truth, some of the kindest and most humane characters I know have displayed their humanity over a plate of pork ribs. So, I must conclude that the whole argument is absurd. Some vegetarians are loving people, and some are not. Same with the meat eaters. Enough! We must learn to get along on the Planet Earth, and we will need one another's support in order to do so.

If the above does not strike you as a theological issue, please reread the first section of the book.

Incidentally, if you are a vegan, a strict vegetarian, you can still use most of the recipes in this book simply by substituting a vegetable stock in the place of the lamb, beef, or chicken stock. I like a brand called George Washington's Seasoning and Broth. It comes in golden and rich brown flavors and contains no animal fat whatsoever. This product does contain MSG, and some people claim that it bothers them. I have used it for years with only positive results, so the choice is up to you. If you want a vegetarian stock without MSG, look for it in a health food store, or make your own. It is quite simple.

Appetizers

It is hard to separate appetizers from the rest of the meal in ancient times. A normal daily meal consisted of bread, olive oil, salt, olives, and perhaps dried fish. Sounds like a cocktail buffet to me!

In more recent times, a first course has become common among the Middle Eastern peoples, and it is a lovely course that is to be eaten amid relaxation and friends as one prepares for the main part of the meal.

Certain portions of the early meal turn up as a first course in our time. Cheese and olives are expected, of course. Hommus (page 108) is common, with several variations. Cut-up fresh vegetables are offered for dipping in the garbanzo paste. Rolled grape leaves (pages 111 and 112) might be found on the serving platter along with bread for dipping and eating. One might even serve a mixed greens salad along with this first plate.

The idea behind this type of first course is based on the need to calm down and relax before eating. It is not considered a separate part of the meal or as "cocktail time." It should function for us as a moment during which we remember that we are about to dine on the beauties of God's Creation. It is the beginning of a blessed time of enjoyment and communicating with friends and family.

So, to the first course!

Hommus
(Garbanzo-Sesame Dip)

Serves 8 to 10 as an appetizer dip

This dip is a basic in the Middle East, and it is very old in terms of food history. While we are using it here for an appetizer, we can also understand how this dish, along with enough bread and wine, could be a whole meal for the desert peoples. I have loved this since I was a child, sitting at the table of my Uncle Victor Abdo.

2 16-ounce cans garbanzo beans (chick-peas)
1/2 cup tahini (find in Middle Eastern markets)
Juice of 1 lemon
2 cloves garlic, crushed

GARNISH

2 tablespoons olive oil
2 tablespoons chopped fresh parsley
Raw vegetables for dipping, such as onion leaves, cucumber slices, fennel bulb pieces, cherry tomatoes, and romaine lettuce leaves
Pita Bread (page 190) for dipping

Drain the juice from 1 can of beans. Place the drained beans in a food processor and add the second can of beans, water and all. Add the tahini, lemon juice, and garlic, and blend until very smooth. Spread onto a plate and top with the garnishes. Serve with the vegetables and pita bread.

Hommus with Dill

Serves 12 as an appetizer dip

Hommus is very versatile. You can do so many things with it and it always seems to cooperate. I like this variation very much. It's best if refrigerated overnight and served the next day. Be sure to have lots of Pita Bread (page 190) on hand. It will disappear rapidly.

Prepare a batch of Hommus (page 108) without the garnish. Place the hommus in a bowl and combine with the following ingredients. Stir together until smooth.

2 tablespoons chopped fresh dill
1 cup plain yogurt, Homemade (page 204) or from the market
Salt and freshly ground black pepper to taste

GARNISH
2 tablespoons olive oil

Serve with vegetables such as onion leaves, cucumber slices, and fennel bulb slices, and pita bread.

Hommus with Sumac and Hyssop

Serves 8 to 10 as an appetizer dip

The addition of these two ancient herbs turns this basic daily dish into a marvelous first course. You could also substitute the same amount of za'atar (page 101) as the garnish.

Prepare a batch of Hommus (page 108) and place it on a serving platter or in a bowl. Sprinkle with the following garnishes and surround the bowl with the vegetables and bread.

GARNISHES

1 teaspoon sumac (page 101)

1 tablespoon chopped fresh hyssop (page 99) or 1 teaspoon dried

2 tablespoons olive oil

Raw vegetables for dipping, such as onion leaves, cucumber slices, and fennel bulb pieces

Pita Bread (page 190) for dipping

Rolled Grape Leaves
with Lamb

Makes about 35 rolls

It is necessary to recognize the fact that many great dishes came out of desperate times. When you have to eat the grape leaves off the vine, you must be in trouble. From that difficult spot came a dish that is now a basic in the diet of the Middle East. Everyone has his or her variation on the filling, but I think you will like this one. It is from my Uncle Vic Abdo.

We have cheated in terms of our commitment to use only food items that were available in Biblical times. We have used rice rather than wheat or barley, and we have added allspice, a flavor that is now common in the Middle East but in fact came from our part of the world, Jamaica. So delicious!

1 16-ounce jar grape leaves in brine (available in
    Middle Eastern markets or delicatessens)
3/4 cup long-grain rice
1 pound lean lamb, coarsely chopped
1/2 teaspoon ground cinnamon, or more to taste
1/2 teaspoon ground allspice, or more to taste
1 teaspoon salt
1/4 teaspoon freshly ground black pepper
Juice of 1 lemon
3 cloves garlic, crushed
1 teaspoon chopped fresh or dried mint leaves
Homemade Yogurt (page 204) for dipping

Remove the grape leaves from the jar and drain.

Rinse the rice, and soak for 3 to 5 minutes in water; drain well.

Mix together the rice, lamb, cinnamon, allspice, salt, and pepper and blend well.

Place a grape leaf on a flat surface, and set 3/4 tablespoon of the lamb and rice filling in the center. Roll into a little bundle with the ends tucked in, as you would wrap a package of meat. Continue making bundles until all the filling has been used.

Place a few of the larger remaining leaves on the bottom of a 3-quart pot. Arrange a layer of the stuffed grape leaves, seam sides down, close together in the pot; they should fit snugly. Place another layer of unfilled leaves on top, and continue to layer the stuffed leaves in the pot, ending with a layer of unfilled leaves. Add water almost to cover. Cover the pot and simmer over medium-low heat for 30 minutes. You might want to use a heat diffuser under the pot for best results.

Blend the lemon juice, garlic, and mint leaves in a 1-cup glass measure. Add enough water to make 1 cup. Pour on top of rolled grape leaves in the pot and replace the lid. Simmer for 30 minutes more. Do not open the lid during this last half hour.

Serve with yogurt for dipping. Can be eaten hot or cold, but generally they are served hot or at room temperature.

Rolled Grape Leaves with Currants and Pine Nuts

Makes 35 rolls

This variation on the old classic is from the Armenian tradition. The rolled grape leaves are rich and sweet and make a cold lunch that is just outstanding. They keep well for a few days and contain no meat and just a little oil. Rather up to date for a recipe that must be one thousand years old.

  1 16-ounce jar grape leaves in brine (available in Middle
      Eastern markets or delicatessens)
  1 cup long-grain rice
  1 cup chopped yellow onions
  2 tablespoons olive oil
  1/4 cup pine nuts

$^1/_2$ **cup dried currants**

2 teaspoons dried dillweed

1 teaspoon salt

$^1/_4$ **teaspoon freshly ground black pepper**

2 tablespoons tomato paste

Juice of 1 lemon

2 cups Chicken Stock (page 118)

Remove the grape leaves from the jar and drain.

Place the rice in a 1-quart saucepan and add 2 cups water. Cover and bring to a boil. Turn off the heat and allow the rice to sit for 10 minutes, then drain.

In a medium frying pan, sauté the onions in 1 tablespoon of the olive oil until clear. Transfer to a bowl.

Toast the pine nuts in the remaining 1 tablespoon olive oil until very light brown. Set aside to cool.

Add the rice, pine nuts, currants, dillweed, salt, and pepper to the onions and mix well.

Place a grape leaf on a flat surface and set $^3/_4$ tablespoon of the rice mixture in the center. Roll up into a little bundle with the ends tucked in, as you would wrap a package or a cigar. Continue making bundles until all the filling has been used.

Place a few of the larger remaining leaves on the bottom of a 3-quart pot. Arrange a layer of stuffed grape leaves, seam sides down, close together in the pot; they should fit snugly. Place another layer of unfilled leaves on top, and continue to layer the stuffed leaves in the pot, ending with a layer of unfilled leaves.

Mix the tomato paste and lemon juice with the chicken stock and pour over the grape leaves. Place a glass plate, upside down, on the top of the leaves. Bring to a simmer over medium-low heat, and simmer for 30 minutes. You might want to use a heat diffuser under the pot for best results. Do not open the lid during the cooking time.

Allow the rolls to cool in the pot, untouched and unopened. Then serve or refrigerate. Serve cold or at room temperature. These are truly delicious.

Yogurt and Cucumber Salad

Serves 6

This is a very common dish in the Middle East and a very old one as well. The Lebanese call this dish *laban* because, I suppose, the yogurt is alive. I hope you make your own yogurt for this. It is well worth the effort.

This dish is fine with the main part of the meal, but it is also commonly served with the first plate, or appetizers.

> 2½ cups plain yogurt, Homemade (page 204) or from
>   the market
> 1 medium cucumber, peeled and seeded
> 2 cloves garlic, crushed
> 1 tablespoon chopped fresh dill
> 2 teaspoons chopped fresh mint
> ½ teaspoon salt
> 1 tablespoon olive oil
> Pita Bread (page 190) for serving

Line a strainer with a couple of layers of cheesecloth and set it over a bowl. Add the yogurt and allow to drain in the refrigerator for 2 hours.

Discard the liquid and place the drained yogurt in the bowl. Coarsely grate the cucumber and add to the bowl. Smash the garlic, dill, mint, and salt together (a mortar and pestle works great for this). Add the oil. Stir into the yogurt and refrigerate overnight.

Serve with pita bread for dipping.

VARIATION: Rub a pinch of saffron between your fingers into a small glass. Stir in 1 teaspoon hot tap water. Stir into the yogurt mixture. This will add a wonderful color and flavor to the salad.

Old World Soups

We tend to underestimate the importance of soups in the ancient world. In our time we serve soup for lunch and sometimes as a first course at a rather formal meal, but soups in early times were basic to the diet of the not so wealthy. They had to make soup out of almost nothing, much as my Grandma Smith used to do. Nothing was wasted and everything eventually ended up in the pot.

None of the following soups has a good deal of meat in it, but we do use good stocks freshly made from bones and vegetables.

We tried hard to stick to basic ingredients, but now and then we strayed into the area of the wealthy, as in delicious Yogurt and Cucumber Soup with Saffron. You have to try that one! All of these soups are easy to prepare if you have stock on hand. Just remember that if you are going to run a first-class kitchen you must make fresh stocks once a week or stock your freezer. The use of instant soup cubes or dry soup powders will certainly not lead you into the realm of grand flavors that fresh stock will offer. Further, instant stuff almost always contains too much salt and who knows what chemicals!

Jewish grandmas seem to have said from the very beginning, "I love you . . . finish your soup!"

Chicken Stock

Makes about 3 quarts

I see no way in which you can get around the use of good basic chicken stock in your kitchen. Bouillon cubes are out of the question and the nearest you can come to good stock from a can is Swanson's or College Inn. Better to make your own. It freezes fine.

The chicken backs and necks are rinsed with hot water so that any traces of blood are removed and the stock will be much clearer. In a kosher kitchen you would salt the pieces of meat and then rinse them.

3 pounds chicken backs and necks

3 quarts cold water

4 ribs celery, coarsely chopped

4 carrots, unpeeled, thickly sliced

2 medium yellow onions, peeled and quartered

8 black peppercorns

Place the chicken backs and necks in a 12-quart soup pot and rinse with very hot tap water. Drain. Add the cold water to the pot, along with the other ingredients. Bring to a simmer, skimming off any foam, and cook gently for 2 hours.

The stock will taste a bit flat to you since it has no salt. Salt will be added when you use the stock in the preparation of soups, sauces, or stews.

Remove the soup from the heat, and when it has cooled a bit, strain the soup through a sieve. Refrigerate or freeze until ready to use.

Lamb Stock

Makes about 3 quarts

Lamb stock is wonderfully versatile. We use it often in recipes and it is simple to make. However, you are going to have to find a butcher who sells a lot of lamb, or a butcher who is willing to order bones for you. It will be worth the effort.

> 3 pounds lamb bones, cut into 1-inch pieces by the butcher
>
> 1 yellow onion, peeled and quartered
>
> 3 ribs celery, coarsely chopped
>
> 2 carrots, unpeeled, chopped
>
> 1 handful fresh parsley, stems and all
>
> 8 black peppercorns

Place the bones in a large stockpot and rinse with very hot tap water. Drain and just cover with fresh cold water (about 3 quarts). Add the vegetables and peppercorns and bring to a simmer. Skim off the froth that forms on the top of the soup. Simmer, covered, for 3 to 4 hours, add the additional water if necessary to keep the bones covered.

Strain the stock, let cool, and chill. The fat will be easy to remove.

The stock will taste a bit flat to you since we have not added salt. Salt will be added when you use the stock in a soup, sauce, or stew.

Beef Stock

Makes about 5 quarts

Meat was rarely eaten in ancient times and the reasons are obvious. Red meat was reserved for High Holy Days, so it was seldom on the table except in the homes of the very wealthy. Further, animals did much of the agricultural work, so few could afford to slaughter and eat them.

When meat was served, however, you can be sure that the bones were saved for soup.

Tell your butcher that you need bare rendering bones. They should not have any meat on them at all, so they should be cheap. Have him saw them into two-inch pieces.

> **5 pounds beef rendering bones, sawed into 2-inch pieces (see headnote)**
>
> **5 quarts cold water**
>
> **1 bunch carrots, unpeeled, chopped**
>
> **1 bunch celery, chopped**
>
> **3 yellow onions, unpeeled, chopped**

Roast the bones in an uncovered pan in a preheated 400° oven for 2 hours. Be careful with this, you don't want your oven to be too hot. Watch the bones; you want them to be a light toasty brown, not black.

Place the roasted bones, along with any grease, in a 20-quart soup pot and add the water, carrots, celery, and onions. (The onion peel will give a lovely color to the stock.)

Bring to a simmer, uncovered, skimming off any foam. Simmer for 12 hours. You will need to add water to keep the liquid up to the same level. Do not salt the stock.

Strain the stock, let cool, and store in the refrigerator. Leave the fat on the top of the stock when you refrigerate it; the fat will seal the stock and allow you to keep it for several days. Beef stock also keeps well in the freezer.

Wheat Soup with Fresh Fennel

Serves 6

This soup is very rich and yet contains no meat whatsoever. It may get a bit too thick for you, so thin it with stock or water. The thickness comes from the cooked grain, which absorbs a lot of liquid. I love this one.

6 cups Chicken Stock (page 118), or more as needed

1 cup coarse-ground bulgur wheat

2 tablespoons olive oil

3 cloves garlic, crushed

1 medium yellow onion, peeled and chopped

1½ cups julienned fennel (1 large, tops discarded)

2 tablespoons chopped fresh parsley

¼ cup plain yogurt, Homemade (page 204) or from the market

Salt and freshly ground black pepper to taste

3 tablespoons butter

Bring the stock and bulgur wheat to a simmer in a 4-quart pot. Meanwhile, heat a medium frying pan and add the oil, garlic, and onion. Sauté for 2 minutes. Add the fennel. Sauté for 3 minutes more.

Add the vegetables to the simmering stock along with the parsley. Bring to a boil and simmer gently, covered, for 45 minutes, until thick. If the soup gets too thick, add some more stock. Stir in the yogurt and salt and pepper to taste. Stir in the butter until melted and serve.

Yogurt and Cucumber Soup with Saffron

Serves 4 to 6

So this one is a little more expensive. I can imagine how wonderful such a dish would taste to the peoples of the desert. Cucumbers were common, as was yogurt. Only the saffron would surprise the common person. Cold soups are wonderful!

> 2 medium cucumbers (about 1¹/₂ pounds), peeled and seeded
>
> 2 cups plain yogurt, Homemade (page 204) or from the market
>
> 1¹/₂ tablespoons chopped fresh dill
>
> 2 teaspoons chopped fresh mint
>
> 1 cup Chicken Stock (page 118)
>
> Pinch of white pepper
>
> Salt to taste
>
> 1 teaspoon saffron

Peel the cucumbers and cut in half lengthwise. Scrape out the seeds with a spoon and discard. Coarsely grate the cucumbers and place in a stainless steel or plastic bowl. Add the remaining ingredients except the saffron.

Rub the saffron between your fingers into a small glass. Add 1 teaspoon of hot tap water and stir with a spoon to release the yellow-orange color. Add to the other ingredients and stir. Cover and refrigerate overnight.

Stir before serving and adjust the salt if necessary. Serve cold.

Lamb Stock, Wheat, and Yogurt Soup

Serves 8 to 10

This soup will taste very rich to you, but note that it has no meat in it. It is the yogurt and bulgur that make it hearty and rich.

1 tablespoon olive oil

2 cloves garlic, crushed

1 medium yellow onion, peeled and diced

8 cups Lamb Stock (page 119)

1 cup coarse-ground bulgur wheat

2 cups plain yogurt, Homemade (page 204) or from the market

Salt and freshly ground black pepper to taste

GARNISH

Chopped fresh parsley or coriander

Heat a 4- to 6-quart pot and add the oil, garlic, and onion. Sauté for 5 minutes. Add the lamb stock. Bring to a boil, cover, and simmer for 1 hour.

Add the bulgur wheat and simmer for 45 minutes more.

Turn off the heat and stir in the yogurt until smooth. Do not boil the soup heavily. Add salt and pepper to taste along with the parsley.

Barley Soup with Vegetables

Serves 8 to 10

This soup is a real stretcher since cooked barley expands to at least four times its size, whereas rice only doubles. Surely this is more delicious than the barley soup of ancient times, but I can only stand so much authenticity . . . and then I have to have flavor!

3/4 cup barley, rinsed and drained

2 tablespoons olive oil

1 medium yellow onion, peeled and thinly sliced

2 cloves garlic, chopped

2 cups julienned fennel

2 cups cleaned and chopped leeks (white part only)

6 1/2 cups Beef Stock (page 120)

2 cups water

1/2 cup dry white wine

Salt and freshly ground black pepper to taste

Place the barley in a 4- to 6-quart pot.

Heat a large frying pan and add the oil, onion, garlic, fennel, and leeks. Sauté for 3 minutes. Add to the pot of barley, along with the stock, water, and wine. Bring to a boil, cover, and simmer gently for 1 1/2 hours, or until the barley is tender. Add salt and pepper to taste.

Onion and Sesame Soup with Coriander

Serves 6 to 8

We know that sesame oil was one of the few oils available in the ancient world, along with olive oil. All oils were expensive, of course, but in this dish the sesame oil is used only for flavor. Be sure to use the dark sesame oil found in Asian markets rather than the clear, light oil found in health food stores.

2 tablespoons olive oil

4 cloves garlic, crushed

8 cups thinly sliced yellow onions

1/2 cup dry white wine

6 cups Chicken Stock (page 118)

1 1/2 cups plain yogurt, Homemade (page 204) or from the market

2 teaspoons toasted sesame oil (find in Asian markets)

2 tablespoons chopped fresh coriander

Salt and freshly ground black pepper to taste

Heat a large frying pan and add the oil, garlic, and onions. Sauté until the onions are tender (you may have to do this in batches). Place the onions in a 4- to 6-quart pot. Deglaze the frying pan with the wine and add to the pot along with the stock. Bring to a boil, reduce the heat, and simmer, covered, for 30 minutes, or until the onion is translucent.

Remove from the heat and stir in the remaining ingredients. Return to the burner just to warm the yogurt; do not boil.

Grains in
Biblical Times

Since meat was seldom eaten in Biblical times and vegetables and fruits were so scarce, it is easy to understand why grains made up the major part of the diet in the early days in Palestine.

Barley and emmer were the most common grains, and bread made from a blend of these two grains was eaten at every meal, every day. Emmer is a rather primitive form of wheat and it can be found in health food shops, along with spelt, another primitive form of wheat. Neither of these two early grains matches the quality of the wheat that we know in our time, a grain that was developed much later in history.

Millet was also used for a form of bread during times of shortages, but this grain was more often used in making a porridgelike dish.

Parched grain, also referred to as crushed grain, is mentioned in the Bible and must be akin to our bulgur wheat, a very old product indeed.

I once said on television that corn as we know it was unknown in Biblical times. I received a note from a lady in the Midwest who was very angry that I, a minister, did not read the Bible more carefully. The Old Testament mentions corn constantly, she said. Well, it is true that the King James translation of the Bible, which was compiled in England in 1611, mentions corn, but not more recent translations. Why? Because the term *corn* in the English spoken at the time referred to any and all grains, just as our term *grain* covers all sorts of cereals. So corn in the Bible does not refer to the American maize, the wonderful grain that originated in this country and was given us by the Native Americans. Maize was given the name corn, or grain, by the English settlers. So, while corn is mentioned in the King James version of the Bible it was not corn as we know it but simply grain. There! Enough!

Since barley and wheat were so common in early times, we have experimented with many ways of cooking these nutritious and versatile cereals. We really should eat more of these grains in our time.

The legumes that were common in Biblical times were two: lentils and garbanzo beans. The Bible uses the word *bean* to refer to garbanzos, or chick-peas, since beans as we know them are from the New World.

So, on to casseroles of barley, and bulgur mixed with lentil sprouts. A very healthy and tasty route to Biblical insight!

Toasted Barley

Parched grain is mentioned in the Bible and it most likely referred to toasting whole grains over a fire. Once they were toasted, they could be hulled and eaten raw or cooked in soups or stews.

When you make a soup, you might want to try adding toasted or parched barley instead of raw. You can toast barley on a cookie sheet in a 400° oven for about ten minutes, or until it barely begins to brown.

A second and much easier way of toasting the grain is to put a bit of grain in a frying pan with just a tiny bit of oil. Shake over medium-high heat until the barley is toasted.

Two-Grain Pilaf
with Lentils

Serves 8 to 10

This simple blend of grains and lentils is right up to the minute in terms of being healthful and politically correct in terms of the concerned dieticians. But, it really is very old. I suggest you try this some weekend when you have time to relax and cook.

1 cup wheat berries (page 101)
2½ teaspoons salt, plus more to taste
1 cup barley
½ cup lentils
2 tablespoons olive oil
2 cloves garlic, chopped
1 medium yellow onion, peeled and chopped
2 tablespoons chopped fresh parsley
Freshly ground black pepper to taste

Soak the wheat berries overnight in ample water to cover.

Drain the wheat and place in a 2-quart pot along with 4 cups water and 1 teaspoon of the salt. Bring to a boil and simmer, covered, for 2 hours, or until tender. Drain and set aside.

Rinse the barley and drain. Place barley in another 2-quart pot with 4 cups cold water and 1 teaspoon of the salt. Bring to a boil and simmer, covered, for 30 minutes, or until the barley is tender. Drain and set aside.

While the barley is cooking, place the lentils in a small pot with 1 cup cold water and the remaining ½ teaspoon salt. Bring to a boil, cover, and simmer for 20 to 25 minutes, or until the lentils are just tender. Drain and set aside.

Heat a large frying pan and add the oil, garlic, and onion. Sauté until the onion is clear. Add the wheat berries, barley, lentils, and parsley. Toss together over medium-high heat for about 3 minutes, until all is tender and hot. Add salt and pepper to taste and toss again.

Baked Barley Casserole

Serves 4 to 6

I would like to think that I can get you and your family hooked on baked barley. It is simple to prepare and it will go with just about anything. You can vary the spices and herbs easily. I love this stuff . . . and it is cheap, of course. Just don't buy barley in those little boxes. Buy it by the plastic bag or, better yet, in bulk in a good delicatessen or health food store. It will save you a great deal of money.

2 tablespoons butter

1 cup barley

2 tablespoons olive oil

2 medium yellow onions, peeled and chopped

Salt and freshly ground black pepper to taste

6 cups Chicken Stock (page 118)

2 teaspoons ground anise

Pinch of ground cinnamon

Melt the butter in a 4-quart stove-top casserole and brown the barley for 2 to 3 minutes. Remove from the heat.

Heat a large frying pan and add the oil and onions. Sauté for 5 minutes, and add to the barley. Add salt and pepper to taste and 3 cups of the stock. Cover and bake in a preheated 350° oven for 1 hour, or until the liquid is almost absorbed.

Add the remaining 3 cups stock, the anise, and cinnamon. Cover and bake for 50 minutes more, or until tender. Adjust salt and pepper to taste.

How to Sprout Grains

I cannot believe the price of sprouted grains in the supermarket produce section! You can sprout them at home with no trouble at all and they will be practically free.

No, I cannot prove that these sprouts were used in Biblical times, but the grains were common and some people must have used them sprouted. In any case, you and I are going to use them because they are delicious!

To start your own sprout factory you will need:

1-quart wide-mouth canning jars with ring lids

1 foot running length plastic screening (available in hardware stores)

Assorted grains for sprouting

For each grain, place ¼ to ½ cup grain in a clean canning jar. Cut a 7-inch square of plastic screening. Wash the screening and place it over the top of the jar. Screw on the ring; no lid is needed. Fill the jar half-full of tepid water and let it sit overnight.

In the morning, drain the jar without removing screening, rinse, and drain again. Rinse the grain and drain once a day until the grain is sprouted to your needs.

Grains vary in terms of the amount of time needed:

Lentils, 3 days

Wheat berries, 3 days

Mung beans, 4 days (these are bean sprouts)

Spelt, soured after 6 days, forget it!

Barley, no success

You can use the screening and jars over and over again. Just wash well after each sprouting and get ready to go again. Use the sprouts in the various recipes in this collection, or come up with your own ideas. How about a sprouted wheat omelette?

Lentils and Garbanzo Beans

Serves 4 to 6 as a side dish

One must suppose that this type of dish, in terms of daily provisions, was as important as salt pork and beans to the American Colonists. Both groups had little else. While the Jews would certainly not eat salt pork, the lesson remains the same. Desperate conditions call for desperate measures.

This desperate measure will fit our time nicely since we are desperate too, in an odd sort of way. Perhaps too *much* food, eh? Well, you will like this dish since it is made rich by the golden raisins and cinnamon. I like it!

1 cup dried garbanzo beans (chick-peas), picked over

2 tablespoons olive oil

1 medium yellow onion, peeled and thinly sliced

1¹/₂ cups lentils

3 cups Chicken Stock (page 118)

¹/₄ cup golden raisins

Pinch of ground cinnamon

1¹/₂ teaspoons salt, or more to taste

Place the garbanzos in a 4-quart saucepan and cover with 3 cups cold water. Bring to a boil. Cover and allow to sit with the burner off for 1 hour.

Add 1 cup more cold water to the garbanzos and bring to a

boil. Simmer, covered, for 1 hour. Drain, discarding the liquid. Return the garbanzos to the pot.

Heat a medium frying pan and add the oil and onion. Sauté for 10 minutes, until the onion is transparent. Add to the garbanzos.

Rinse the lentils in cold water and drain. Add the lentils to the pot of garbanzos along with the stock, raisins, cinnamon, and salt. Bring to a boil, cover, and simmer gently for 25 to 35 minutes, until all is tender. Salt to taste if necessary.

Lentils and Barley

Serves 6 to 8

I can just hear some of you saying, "Why, this dish has no meat in it. The Frug has gone vegetarian on us!" No, we are talking about what was eaten during Biblical times. I am not a vegetarian, but I have vegetarian recipes in all of my books. I am convinced that we depend upon meat too much for flavor in our diet. Serve this dish with some vegetables and you will be surprised. It is very good.

2 tablespoons butter

1 cup barley, rinsed and drained

2 tablespoons olive oil

2 medium yellow onions, peeled and chopped

6 cups Chicken Stock (page 118)

2 tablespoons chopped fresh parsley

2 cups lentils, rinsed and drained

1 teaspoon salt, plus more to taste

Freshly ground black pepper to taste

GARNISH

Extra virgin olive oil

Heat a 4- to 6-quart ovenproof casserole. Add the butter and barley and lightly brown the barley. Remove from the heat.

Heat a large frying pan. Add the oil and sauté the onions for 5 minutes. Add to the barley. Add 3 cups of the stock along with the parsley, cover, and place in a preheated 350° oven. Bake for about 1 hour, until the liquid is almost absorbed.

In the meantime, place the lentils in a separate pot with 6 cups cold water and the salt. Bring to a boil and boil for about 20 minutes, until just tender. Drain and set aside.

Add the remaining 3 cups stock to the barley and bake for 30 minutes more. Stir in the cooked lentils and bake for 10 minutes more. Add salt and pepper to taste. Drizzle with the oil.

Wheat Berries and Garbanzo Beans with Artichokes

Serves 6 to 8

Yes, this one is a tad unusual. Artichokes were known in Biblical times, but we can be sure the vegetable was nothing like that which we know in our time. Since artichokes are actually thistles, I assume that the artichoke of Biblical days was a wild thistle and simply harvested on the desert.

This really works very well, although Craig and I were somewhat suspicious when we thought it up. It uses desert ingredients but it speaks of a dish thought up by one of those New York cooks who try to blend the New World with the Old. Why not?

1½ cups dried garbanzo beans (chick-peas)

1½ cups wheat berries (page 101)

2 tablespoons olive oil

1 medium yellow onion, peeled and diced

2 medium artichokes, cleaned (see Note) and sliced lengthwise into ¼-inch slices

1 lemon, cut in half (for rubbing the artichokes; see Note)

2 tablespoons chopped fresh parsley

Salt and freshly ground black pepper to taste

3 cups Chicken Stock (page 118)

GARNISH

Extra virgin olive oil

Place the garbanzo beans, wheat berries, and 2 quarts water in a 4- to 6-quart pot. Bring to a boil and simmer, covered, for 1 hour and 30 minutes. Turn off the burner and allow to stand, covered, for 15 minutes. Drain the beans, return to the pot, and set aside, covered.

Heat a large frying pan and add the oil and onions. Sauté for 2 minutes. Add the artichokes and parsley and sauté for 10 minutes. Add salt and pepper to taste. Add to the garbanzos and wheat berries, along with the stock. Bring to a boil, cover and simmer for 30 minutes or until all is tender. Add salt and pepper to taste and drizzle with extra virgin olive oil.

Cleaning an Artichoke

Break off the first two or three layers of the lower leaves. Using a paring knife, cut off the top half of the remaining leaves: Do this by holding the artichoke on its side, cutting down on an angle away from the stem. Turn the choke as you cut until the purple thistle center is exposed. Using a grapefruit spoon, remove the purple center, exposing the meaty artichoke bottom. Cut off the stem, leaving about an inch intact. Trim off the tough exterior skin of the stem. Rub the whole choke with fresh lemon juice to prevent discoloring.

You are now ready to cook it!

Wheat Berries with Onions and Mint

Serves 3 to 4 as a side dish

You have to do this dish on a day when you are doing a lot of quiet and relaxing cooking, since the dish takes three hours to prepare. For wheat? Yes, but you can substitute bulgur for the wheat berries and do the whole thing in less than half an hour. However, now and then it is fun to do things the old way. This helps us better understand the early flavors and it demands that we understand how much work it was to cook in the ancient world.

1 cup wheat berries (page 101) (find in health food stores)

3 cups Chicken Stock (page 118)

1 cup thinly sliced yellow onion

1 tablespoon olive oil

Salt and freshly ground black pepper to taste

GARNISH

1 tablespoon chopped fresh mint or parsley

Place the wheat in a 2-quart heavy saucepan and add 4 cups water. Cover, bring to a boil, and simmer for 2 minutes. Turn off the heat, leaving the covered pan on the stove, untouched, for 2 hours.

Drain the wheat, return to the pan, and add the chicken stock. Bring to a simmer, cover, and cook until tender, about 1 hour.

In the meantime sauté the onion in the olive oil just until clear. Remove from the heat.

Five minutes before the wheat is finished, add the onion. Add salt and pepper to taste. Garnish with the mint or parsley.

Wheat Berries with Garlic and Dill

Serves 4 to 6

Just read the recipe and you will understand the Biblical flavors here. Garlic and dill must have been a most popular combination. In this dish, it is very comfortable.

1 cup wheat berries (page 101) (find in health food stores)

3 cups Chicken Stock (page 118), or more as needed

3 cloves garlic, crushed

2 tablespoons chopped fresh dill

Salt to taste

Soak the wheat berries overnight in ample water to cover.

Drain the wheat berries and place in a 2-quart pot. Add the stock and garlic and bring to a boil. Cover and simmer gently for 2 hours, or until tender. You will probably have to add additional water or stock if the pot dries out too much. Stir occasionally until the wheat is tender.

Stir in the dill and add salt to taste.

Bulgur Wheat Pilaf
with Leeks

Serves 4 to 6 as a side dish

Such a replacement for potatoes or rice! Bulgur is so easy to cook and this dish is so enlivened with spices that I know that your family will think you a genius.

1/4 cup olive oil

1 cup coarse-ground bulgur wheat

2 cups cleaned chopped leeks (about 3 medium leeks, white part only)

2 cups Chicken Stock (page 118)

1 1/2 teaspoons ground coriander

Pinch of ground cinnamon

1 teaspoon salt, or more to taste

2 teaspoons chopped fresh mint

Heat a medium frying pan and add 2 tablespoons of the oil. Toast the bulgur over medium heat for 3 minutes. Remove to a 2- to 4-quart pot. Trim off the green tops and the core ends of the leeks and discard. Chop the white part of the leeks coarsely and place in a colander. Rinse well with cold water and drain.

Add the remaining oil to the frying pan. Add the leeks and sauté for 2 minutes. Set aside on a plate to cool.

Add the stock, coriander, cinnamon, and salt to the pot of bulgur. Bring to a boil, cover, and simmer for 10 minutes. Add the sautéed leeks and mint and cook, covered, for 10 to 12 minutes more, until the bulgur is just tender. Add salt to taste if necessary.

Bulgur Wheat Pilaf
with Mulberries

Serves 4 to 6 as a side dish

We do not generally think of cooking grain with berries. We should. It was done by Biblical peoples and by the Native Americans of our land. It is not as sweet as it sounds and it will be a hit with the kids. Anything to get them to eat more grains! If you cannot find dried mulberries, you can substitute ½ cup blackberries along with ½ cup raspberries. The resulting flavor will not be too far from the old desert mulberries. You might add 1 tablespoon of fresh lemon juice if you use fresh berries. You will need the tartness.

> ³/₄ **cup dried mulberries (find in Middle Eastern markets)**
>
> ¹/₂ **cup tepid (110° to 115°) water**
>
> **2 tablespoons olive oil**
>
> **1¹/₂ cups coarse-ground bulgur wheat**
>
> **2 cups Chicken Stock (page 118)**
>
> **Salt and freshly ground black pepper to taste**

Place the mulberries in a small bowl with the water. Allow to soak for 30 minutes, then drain.

Heat a small saucepan and add the oil and bulgur. Toast the bulgur in the oil for a few minutes, but don't burn. Add the chicken stock and bring to a boil. Cover and simmer gently for 15 minutes. Stir in the drained mulberries and cook, covered, for 5 minutes more, until bulgur is tender. Add salt and pepper to taste.

Sprouted Grain Pilaf

Sprouted grains are delicious when added to pilaf dishes. Simply stir the sprouts into any finished pilaf dish at the last minute. This recipe may seem like something from a health food store, but the sprouts really do add an interesting texture and refreshing flavor to your side dish. See page 134 for tips on sprouting grains.

Lentil and Wheat Pilaf

Serves 6 as a side dish

Wheat and lentils can stand on their own as a very good meal. Lentils are the most nutritious legume that we know, and wheat has been a blessing to us since the beginning of history. Your family will take to this dish, I promise.

1 cup lentils

3 cups water

2½ teaspoons salt, or more to taste

2 tablespoons olive oil

1½ cups coarse-ground bulgur wheat

3 cups Chicken Stock (page 118)

¼ cup chopped fresh parsley

1 tablespoon butter

Freshly ground black pepper to taste

Place the lentils in a small bowl and cover with the cold water. Allow to soak for 1 hour, then drain.

Place the lentils in a small pot and add 3 cups water and 1½ teaspoons of the salt. Bring to a boil and simmer, covered, for 10 minutes. Drain the lentils and set aside.

Heat the pot again and add the oil and bulgur wheat. Toast the bulgur in the oil until lightly browned. Add the chicken stock and remaining 1 teaspoon salt. Bring to a boil and simmer, cov-

Hommus with Sumac and Hyssop (page 110)

Clockwise from top left: Almonds, Millet, Spelt,
Bulgur, Barley, Pistachios, Walnuts

Yogurt and Cucumber Soup with Saffron (page 122)

Clockwise from top left: Garlic, Bay Leaves, Mustard
Seed, Capers, Black Caraway, Sumac, Hyssop, Saffron

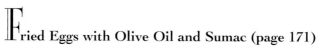

Fried Eggs with Olive Oil and Sumac (page 171)

Top to bottom: Desert Flat Bread (Pita or Pocket Bread) (page 190), Coarse Wheat Bread (page 194), Semolina Bread (page 197), Fennel Bread (page 189), Four-Grain Bread with Lentils (page 184)

ogurt Cheese (page 206)

Grilled Lamb Chops with Mint and Cinnamon
in Grape Leaves (page 226), Barley with
Saffron and Grapes (page 148)

F owl Stuffed with Bulgur Wheat Dressing (page 244),
Fried Cucumbers with Sumac (page 275)

Roasted Chicken with Quince Glaze (page 254),
Fried Lentil Cakes (page 147),
Sautéed Onions and Leeks (page 269)

Chicken with Olives and Leeks (page 252),
Leek Fritters with Garlic (page 272)

Broiled Fish with Garlic and Mint (page 261),
Barley Salad (page 153)

Yogurt Cheese with Herbs (page 207), Pita (page 190),
Rolled Grape Leaves with Lamb (page 111)

Biblical Fruit Salad (page 162)

Sesame and Almond Honey Candy (page 281)

 Honey Cake (page 282)

ered, for 10 minutes. Stir in the lentils, parsley, and butter. Cover and cook for 5 to 10 minutes more, until all is tender and the liquid is absorbed. Add salt and pepper to taste.

Barley Casserole with Leeks, Onions, and Sesame Oil

Serves 6

These barley recipes may tend to sound alike, since we have prepared so many, but I promise you they will not taste alike. Barley was so common in Biblical times that it is fun to experiment with endless possibilities. This dish is rather rich and very good.

 2 tablespoons olive oil
 1 cup barley
 1 medium yellow onion, peeled and chopped
 4 cups Beef Stock (page 120)
 2 cups water
 4 cups cleaned coarsely chopped leeks (white part only)
 1 tablespoon toasted sesame oil
 Salt and freshly ground black pepper to taste

Heat a large frying pan and add 1 tablespoon of the oil and the barley. Lightly brown the barley, and remove to a 4- to 6-quart ovenproof casserole.

Heat the frying pan again and add the remaining 1 tablespoon oil and the onion. Sauté until the onion is just tender. Add to the casserole. Combine the beef stock and water and add 3 cups of this liquid to the pot. Cover and bake in a preheated 350° oven for about 1 hour, or until the liquid is almost absorbed.

Add the remaining stock mix, the cleaned leeks, and sesame oil. Continue baking, covered, until all the liquid is absorbed, about 45 minutes more. Add salt and pepper to taste.

Esau's Pottage

Serves 6 to 8

Lentils are a very old vegetable, going back to pre-Biblical times. In the Book of Genesis, Esau comes upon his brother, Jacob, who is cooking a pottage of lentils. Esau is hungry, and in order to get to the lentils, he agrees to give Jacob his birthright. I assume that must have been some dish of lentils! This is the recipe Esau gave me, so it is genuine, and it was a long-distance phone call! Serve as a side dish on almost any menu.

2 cups lentils

4 cups Chicken Stock (page 118)

2 cups thinly sliced yellow onions

1 tablespoon olive oil

3 tablespoons toasted sesame oil

Salt to taste

Soak the lentils in a bowl with the chicken stock for 3 hours at room temperature.

Place the lentils and stock in a pot, bring to a simmer, and simmer for about 1 hour, or until the lentils are barely tender.

Meanwhile, heat a frying pan. Sauté the onions in the olive oil until they are clear. Add the sesame oil and salt. Place all of the ingredients in a baking casserole, and bake, covered, in a preheated 325° oven for about 1 hour, until most of the stock has been absorbed.

Fried Lentil Cakes

Makes about 6 cakes

I cannot believe that, given the scarcity of food in Biblical times, food was thrown out or wasted as we do in our time. In an effort to figure out what to do with some leftover lentil pottage, I came up with this recipe. It is very good indeed. Even the Innkeeper in Old Jerusalem would be impressed with this one, and he did not even serve food!

> 1 large egg, beaten
>
> 1/2 cup fine bread crumbs
>
> 2 cups Esau's Pottage (page 146), cold
>
> Salt and freshly ground black pepper to taste
>
> 3 tablespoons olive oil for frying
>
> Flour for dusting

Beat the egg in a bowl and stir in the bread crumbs until they have absorbed the liquid. Stir into the prepared cold pottage and salt and pepper to taste. Form the mixture into round patties 4 inches wide and 1/2 inch thick.

Heat a large nonstick frying pan and add the oil. Lightly coat the patties with flour and panfry for about 3 minutes on each side, until nicely browned. (Turn the patties carefully while cooking as they are very tender.)

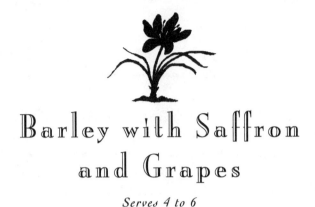

Barley with Saffron and Grapes

Serves 4 to 6

What is barley doing running around with the flavors of the Arabian nights? Taste this one and you will understand. It is a bit rich.

My wife, Patty, spent a good deal of her childhood in Saudi Arabia. This is the kind of dish that makes her remember good and tasty times.

1 tablespoon olive oil

1 large yellow onion, peeled and diced

1½ cups barley, rinsed and drained

5 cups Chicken Stock (page 118)

½ teaspoon saffron

⅓ cup slivered almonds, toasted

2 cups seedless green grapes

¼ cup chopped fresh coriander

½ teaspoon ground cumin

Salt and freshly ground black pepper to taste

Heat a 4- to 6-quart pot and add the oil and onion. Sauté for 5 minutes. Add the drained barley and sauté for 5 minutes. Add the chicken stock and saffron. Bring to a boil, cover, and simmer for 45 minutes.

Meanwhile, toast the almonds in a dry frying pan over low heat until golden brown.

Add the almonds to the pot along with the grapes, coriander, and cumin. Simmer for 15 minutes more. Add salt and pepper to taste.

Salads from the
Ancient World

All of the salads in this chapter are made with ingredients that could be found in Palestine two thousand years ago. However, everything was seasonal, of course, so it must have been very difficult to find fresh ingredients for much of the year. Certainly there was no lettuce of any kind, and as you can see from the vegetable list on page 95, most vegetables would have been cooked.

I think you will like these ancient flavors, even if I am pushing my luck a bit. In our time, we simply refuse to eat dinner without a salad . . . so good luck with these.

Sesame Paste Dressing

Makes about 1 cup

This refreshing dressing can be used on any number of vegetables. You can certainly use ¹/₂ tablespoon tahini (page 101) in place of the toasted seeds, but the following method will give you the best flavor.

2 tablespoons sesame seeds

¹/₂ cup extra virgin olive oil

1 tablespoon white wine vinegar

1 tablespoon fresh lemon juice

1 tablespoon coarsely grated yellow onion

Small pinch of sugar

1 teaspoon toasted sesame oil (find in Asian markets)

Salt and freshly ground black pepper to taste

Toast the sesame seeds in a small frying pan over low heat until golden brown. Allow to cool and coarsely grind (use a mortar and pestle for this or a small electric spice or coffee grinder).

In a small bowl, whisk together the oil, vinegar, and lemon juice. Whisk in the sesame seeds and remaining ingredients until smooth. Use immediately or refrigerate.

Barley Salad

Serves 6 to 8 as a salad course

Since barley was a common grain in Biblical times, it makes sense that it would wind up in a salad; or at least certainly in our time. This is actually very delicious. It is a variation on a recipe from an interesting book entitled *The Garden of Eden Cookbook* (see Bibliography).

1 cup barley, rinsed and drained

¹/₂ cup olive oil

3 tablespoons fresh lemon juice

³/₄ cup chopped fresh parsley

³/₄ cup chopped fresh dill

¹/₂ cup chopped green onions

Salt and freshly ground black pepper to taste

Lettuce cups for serving

Line a steamer basket with cheesecloth so the barley will not fall through, and spread the barley in the basket. Cover and steam until tender, about 2 hours. You may have to add more water to your steamer.

Place the hot barley in a medium bowl. Whisk together the olive oil and lemon juice and add to the barley. Add the remaining ingredients except the lettuce cups and stir gently to combine. Refrigerate for 1 to 2 hours.

Serve the salad in lettuce cups.

Barley Salad with
Fresh Fennel and Sumac

Serves 6

The addition of sumac, that wonderful sour and woody spice, gives this salad a wonderful lift. I could eat this often.

1¹/₂ cups barley, rinsed and drained

1 teaspoon salt

1 cup thinly sliced white onion

1 cup finely julienned fennel

1 tablespoon sumac (page 101)

¹/₄ cup chopped fresh parsley

DRESSING

²/₃ cup extra virgin olive oil

1¹/₂ tablespoons fresh lemon juice

1 tablespoon white wine vinegar

Salt and freshly ground black pepper to taste

Lettuce cups for serving

Place the barley in a 4-quart pot and add 8 cups cold water and the salt. Bring to a boil and simmer, covered, for 35 to 40 minutes, or until tender but still firm. Drain well and spread the barley out onto a baking sheet to cool.

Place the barley in a bowl along with the onion, fennel, sumac, and parsley.

Mix the ingredients for the dressing together and add to the bowl. Toss together. Cover and allow to marinate for at least 4 hours in the refrigerator. Toss the salad occasionally while chilling.

Serve in lettuce cups.

Cucumber Salad with Mixed Fresh Herbs

Serves 6

This is what you might call a "New Pickle Salad." Perfect at any time of the year, and it reminds us of the frustration that the Children of Israel felt while fleeing Egypt: "At least in Egypt we had onions and garlic and cucumbers."

4 medium cucumbers (2 pounds), peeled and thinly sliced

1½ teaspoons salt

1 tablespoon chopped fresh parsley

1 tablespoon chopped fresh dill

1 tablespoon chopped fresh mint

¾ cup thinly sliced yellow onion

1 clove garlic, crushed

¼ cup extra virgin olive oil

2 tablespoons distilled white vinegar

Freshly ground black pepper to taste

Place the cucumbers in a colander. Toss with the salt and allow to drain into a bowl for 1 hour. Carefully toss the cucumbers a couple of times while draining.

Discard the liquid that has accumulated and place the cucumbers in the bowl. Toss with the remaining ingredients. Chill for at least 3 hours. Toss the salad once while chilling. You probably won't need any additional salt.

Cucumber Salad
with Dill and Hyssop

Serves 4 to 6

Dried hyssop will work fine in this dish. It comes back to life
with the oil and vinegars. I am sure that this mixture was known
to just about everyone in Palestine two thousand years ago.

> 2 large cucumbers (about 1½ pounds)
>
> ½ cup olive oil
>
> 1 tablespoon white wine vinegar
>
> 1 tablespoon chopped fresh dill
>
> 1 tablespoon fresh lemon juice
>
> 2 teaspoons dried hyssop (page 99), rubbed between
> your fingers

Partially peel the cucumbers lengthwise, leaving some strips
of green outer skin for color. Using a mandoline, thinly slice the
cucumbers into a bowl. (You can also use the slicing side of a
stainless steel box grater or any vegetable cutter that will give
you thin slices.)

In a large bowl, mix together the remaining ingredients. Add
the cucumbers and toss together. Cover and chill for 2 hours.

Cucumber Salad with Onions and Fresh Hyssop

Serves 4 to 6

I planted a batch of fresh hyssop out in my herb garden. It is easy to grow and has a very different flavor, sort of a cross between mint, anise, and thyme. When I talked to my friend Cathy Wilkinson Barash, author of a wonderful book entitled *Edible Flowers: From Garden to Palate* (see Bibliography), I told her I was growing hyssop. "Make cucumber salad," said she, so here it is. Very refreshing.

Incidentally, in Biblical times, hyssop was used not only as a food but also as a ritual cleansing herb and as a medicine.

2 medium cucumbers (about 1 pound)

1 cup thinly sliced yellow onion

⅓ cup olive oil

1 teaspoon honey

2 tablespoons white wine vinegar

2 tablespoons chopped fresh hyssop (page 99)

Salt and freshly ground black pepper to taste

Slice the cucumbers thinly with the skin on. Place in a bowl with the onion. Combine the remaining ingredients in a small bowl and whisk together until smooth. Add to the cucumbers and onions and toss together. Cover the bowl and allow to marinate in the refrigerator for 2 hours.

Lentil Sprout Salad with Sesame Paste Dressing

Serves 6

We had to cheat on this salad, since it really does need some lettuce. Can you imagine how difficult it must have been to grow greens on the desert? Lettuce was out of the question, but in this dish it is perfect.

> 1 head romaine or iceberg lettuce, separated into leaves, washed, and dried
>
> ½ cup lentils, sprouted (page 134; this will take about 3 days)
>
> ½ cup Sesame Paste Dressing (page 152), or more to taste
>
> Salt and freshly ground black pepper (optional)

Place the lettuce in a large bowl. Add the lentil sprouts and toss with the dressing. Season with salt and pepper if desired.

Tabbouleh

Serves 6 to 8 as a salad course

I am sure that this salad is very old, but when you remove the later additions to it, those foods that were not around in ancient Palestine, you come up with a whole new version. . . . No, make that a whole old version.

1 cup fine-grain bulgur wheat

2 large bunches parsley

2 bunches scallions, cut into large pieces

2 tablespoons coarsely chopped fresh mint or 1 teaspoon dried mint

1/4 cup extra virgin olive oil

1/4 cup fresh lemon juice

1/4 teaspoon ground cinnamon, or more to taste

1 teaspoon salt

1/4 teaspoon freshly ground black pepper

Soak the bulgur wheat in 2 cups cold water for 15 minutes. Drain and squeeze dry.

Pick the parsley leaves from the large stems. Wash at least twice and drain very well. Mix the parsley, scallions, and mint together. Place in a food processor fitted with the metal blade and pulse until finely chopped. Place in a large mixing bowl.

In another bowl, combine the olive oil, lemon juice, cinnamon, salt, and pepper. Whisk or stir with a fork until smooth. Add to the parsley mixture and mix thoroughly. Serve immediately.

NOTE: The amounts of all the ingredients can be varied to taste. More contemporary versions common in the Middle East in our time might add chopped red bell pepper, chopped celery, chopped tomatoes, and a bit of allspice. Make it the old way first, and then you might want to add these newer items.

Blanched Leek Salad

Serves 6

Leeks were important in Biblical times and I suspect rather common. This salad of wilted or blanched leeks is based on foods available at the time, with the exception of the romaine lettuce. Craig, our chef, decided that lettuce is necessary to this dish, so we cheated. It is delicious.

8 cups julienned leeks (5 to 6 medium leeks, white part only)

1 tablespoon olive oil

DRESSING

⅓ cup extra virgin olive oil

1 tablespoon fresh lemon juice

1 tablespoon white wine vinegar

Salt and freshly ground black pepper to taste

1 medium head romaine lettuce, torn into pieces, washed, and dried

Cut off the root end of the leek and discard. Trim off the dark green tops of the leeks and discard. Slice the white part of the leeks lengthwise and julienne about ¼ inch thick.

Bring a 12-quart pot of water to a rapid boil and add the oil. Blanch the leeks for 20 seconds and drain. Plunge into a large bowl of cold water, drain well, and place in a large bowl.

Combine the ingredients for the dressing and toss with the drained leeks. Marinate overnight in the refrigerator.

Serve the salad over torn romaine lettuce.

Cold Leek Salad with Sesame Paste Dressing

Serves 6

This is so easy and a bit unusual. It will be no trouble to make, particularly if you prepare a couple of batches of sesame salad dressing ahead of time.

Prepare the leeks as for Blanched Leek Salad (page 160), omitting the dressing. Toss with $1/3$ cup Sesame Paste Dressing (page 152), cover, and refrigerate for several hours. Toss the salad a couple of times while chilling.

Biblical Fruit Salad

Serves 12

When I drew up the list of fruits that were available in the ancient world, this salad seemed like a natural. But after I relaxed in the summer sun and ate a bowl of it, I realized that you would have had to have been a member of the priestly or ruling class in order to afford this dish. Now we can have fresh fruit almost year-round, and we think nothing of it. Seasons no longer seem to matter, and I think we have lost more than just the seasons in this change. There is something to be said for looking forward to a special fruit season and waiting with anticipation for those fruits that are not grown in a hothouse. Now, on to the recipe. When you make this, please remember how wealthy we really are in this culture.

> 1/2 **pound dried figs**
> 1/2 **pound dried apricots**
> 1/4 **cup brandy**
> 2 **tablespoons butter**
> 3 **cups cantaloupe cut into** 1 1/2-**inch pieces**
> 6 **cups watermelon cut into** 1 1/2-**inch pieces**
> 4 **cups honeydew melon cut into** 1 1/2-**inch pieces**
> 2 **cups seedless red grapes**
> 1/4 **cup sweet Marsala wine**

Place the figs and apricots in a small bowl and cover with warm water. Allow to soak for 1 hour. Drain.

Cut the figs in half and return to the bowl along with the apricots. Add the brandy and allow to soak for 30 minutes. Strain the fruit, reserving the brandy.

Melt the butter in a medium frying pan and sauté the figs and apricots until lightly browned. Deglaze the pan with the reserved brandy, and simmer a couple minutes until the liquid is almost evaporated. Remove the figs and apricots, along with the brandy, to a bowl and let cool.

Place the remaining fruit in a large bowl and add the cooled fruit with the brandy. Add the Marsala and stir well. Allow to chill for 1 hour, stirring the salad one more time.

Eggs on the
Biblical Table

Funny how we assume that something we have always known must have been around forever. Not so with the egg. Domesticated fowl were not even known until about the fifth century B.C., or even later. However, wild bird eggs were gathered prior to that time, and once a fowl became domesticated, eggs became more common. They were familiar by New Testament times. Just as is true with every other animal that was common in Biblical times, it is doubtful that anyone would kill the egg source and eat her. Not likely at all. As Patty, my wife, puts it, "Eggs came before chicken soup." She is right, of course.

The recipes in this section are typical of the way that eggs have been cooked since ancient times and still are in our time in the Middle East. There are old rabbinical references that point to the fact that eggs were boiled or fried in oil in early days. Not much difference in terms of methods in our time.

I have offered you only four egg dishes in this section, and please do not ask me which is my favorite. I cannot decide. You can use these dishes as they were used in ancient times, at any meal of the day.

Eggs with Yogurt and Garlic

Serves 1 to 2

This dish was common in the ancient world and is still very popular in Turkey and Greece. Be sure that the pan is not too hot when you put in the eggs, as you want to avoid that terrible tough edge that one gets on a fried egg when the pan is too hot. On the other hand, don't cook these so slowly that the yolks get hard. This is good for any meal of the day, as it must have been in early times.

½ cup plain yogurt, Homemade (page 204) or from
the market

2 cloves garlic, crushed

2 teaspoons olive oil

3 large eggs

Salt and freshly ground black pepper to taste

Pita bread (page 190) for serving

Combine the yogurt and garlic and set aside.

Heat an 8-inch nonstick frying pan and add the oil. Crack the eggs into the pan and season with salt and pepper to taste. Top with the yogurt and cook, covered, over low heat for about 3 minutes; don't overcook. Serve with pita bread.

Scrambled Eggs
with Lamb

Serves 3 for breakfast

When I was a child, my Uncle Vic, who is Lebanese, would cook this for me. He had chickens during World War II, when the rest of us could not even buy eggs. Well, Uncle Vic had eggs! Dear Aunt Tessie would invite me to come and stay with them for a week or so during the summer . . . and there we had the most wonderful vacation a little kid could imagine. Tessie made me egg sandwiches and Uncle Vic made this dish.

Vic's ancestral land, Lebanon, was the land of the Phoenicians in the Bible. His parents cooked eggs this way and I assume that their parents' parents cooked them the same way. I absolutely love this simple dish of scrambled eggs with lamb and spices. I have cheated a bit in terms of this recipe collection, since allspice was not common in Biblical times, but you will love it in this dish.

2 tablespoons olive oil

1 cup diced boneless lamb steak meat (small dice)
(save the bone for soup stock)

1/2 cup chopped yellow onion

Salt and freshly ground pepper to taste

Pinch of ground allspice

Pinch of ground cinnamon

6 large eggs, lightly beaten (do not add any water to
your eggs)

Heat a 10-inch frying pan and add the oil and lamb. Lightly brown the lamb. Add the onion and sauté until the onion is just tender. Add the remaining ingredients. Turn and fold the eggs over medium-low heat until scrambled. Do not overcook.

Scrambled Eggs with Dill and Yogurt Cheese

Serves 2 to 3

This rather rich dish blends two favorite flavors from the ancient world, yogurt and dill. I suppose you would have to have been a very serious cook to come up with this in the old days, but there is no reason why we should not enjoy it now.

1 tablespoon olive oil

6 large eggs, beaten

1 tablespoon chopped fresh dill

$^1/_3$ cup Yogurt Cheese (page 206)

Salt and freshly ground black pepper to taste

Heat a 10-inch nonstick frying pan and add the oil and beaten eggs. Cook over medium-low heat, stirring all the time, until no longer runny but still very soft. Add the dill and yogurt cheese and fold together until the eggs are set. Add salt and pepper to taste.

Fried Eggs with Olive Oil and Sumac

Serves 2 for breakfast as this is very rich

This is another dish from my childhood offered me by my Uncle Vic Abdo. When I offered it to my own sons, they could not quite get the pronunciation of sumac, so they called the dish eggs and cement! We had great fun when they would invite tiny friends to stay over for the night and then have eggs and cement for breakfast.

This is just luscious! Do not let the oil get too hot, or the edges of the eggs will get crispy.

4 large eggs

3 tablespoons extra virgin olive oil

1 teaspoon sumac (page 101) (find in Middle Eastern markets)

Salt and freshly ground black pepper to taste

Warm Pita Bread (page 190) for sopping

Crack the eggs into a small bowl, making sure not to break the yolks. Heat a 10-inch frying pan over medium heat and add the oil. Add the eggs and sprinkle on the sumac and salt and pepper to taste. Cover and cook over low heat until the egg whites are set but the yolks are still runny. Serve with warm pita bread for sopping.

Bread in
Early Times

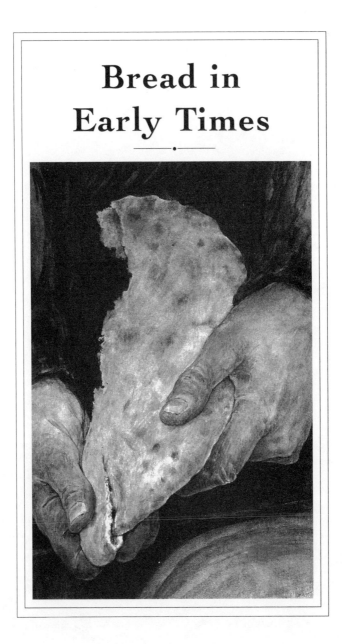

B read is one of the oldest foods that we know, a delicious creation celebrated by cultures all over the globe. The variations on the common theme of ground grain made into a dough and cooked range from the tortillas of Mexico to the fancy raised egg loaves of France. One of the oldest forms of bread that we know goes back to the Middle Eastern desert.

The Children of Israel developed a yeast that seems to be common in the air in certain parts of the desert. From this yeast came the first raised loaves and then yogurt and cheese. Wine, of course, has its own yeast, which develops on the outside of the grapes. So yeast gives us some of our most precious food products, wine and bread and cheese. All of these seem to have come from the desert. I think yeast is one of the Holy One's most clever creations. Robert Farrar Capon claims that yeast is "the thumbprint of the Creator" (see Bibliography).

When the Jews left captivity in Egypt, they left behind them the legacy of leavening. Before the Jews, the Egyptians had been baking a very firm unleavened loaf that had to be soaked in water before it could be eaten. By the way, at some point the water that drained off the soaked bread fermented, and thus the Egyptians are credited with the invention of beer!

The unleavened bread called the matzo came about when Moses told the Jews to leave their leavening behind them when they fled Egypt. Certainly the leavening would not live while the Children of Israel were running like mad across the desert. Instead of raised loaves, they learned to bake unleavened bread, the matzo. Since leavening can become infected with an outside or foreign fungi, kosher law, which refers to clean and perfect in terms of Jewish ritual, requires that one's home be completely cleansed each year in preparation for Passover. At that time no leavening or even flour from the past year can remain in the house. Even flour can become infected. So, matzo, matzo meal, and matzo cake meal, which have all been made under very clean and carefully regulated conditions, are used during this special time of Passover. For the Jews even the eating of bread becomes an act of worship and commitment.

The Greeks were wonderful bread bakers, and they were probably the first to put spices and seeds in bread. This glorious new touch came into the Roman kitchen when the Greek cooks were taken into Roman slavery. Their bread ideas were then spread throughout the rest of the ancient world.

The breads in this collection of recipes are all based on breads of the ancient world in one form or another. The Yogurt-Raised Wheat Bread will surely surprise you. The Raised Barley Loaf is wonderful, and my mother loves toast made from the Sprouted Wheat Bread.

One more thing before we get started. Bread baking takes a bit of commitment and patience. It is also a holy act as far as I am concerned. The practice of placing the seed in the womb of Mother Earth was always an act of worship in the ancient world. If you simply buy bread from the market, it seems to me that you miss out on a wonderful part of our spiritual journey. Bread.

Hints on Baking Bread

1. Get your hands into the dough. There is something holy about baking bread, about mixing the grain from the earth with the yeast from the desert winds, a Biblical symbol for the breath of God. Bread is one of the oldest foods in the world, and there is also something holy in smelling the yeast as it brings the heavy and pasty dough into the realm of a light and luscious loaf. And kneading is a blessing to your mental health. Your grandmother used to bake bread all the time, and she never saw a psychiatrist! When she was upset, she went to the kitchen and beat the blazes out of a batch of bread dough . . . and the bread was wonderful. So was Grandma!

I find an electric bread machine to be a gadget designed to take all of the joy out of baking bread.

2. In the ancient world, one never used bread pans. The bread was baked on bricks or oven stones. While I do have a few recipes in this section that I found easier with bread pans, most of the breads are best when baked on tiles. You can find pizza stones or oven tiles for your oven in any good gourmet shop. Simply place the tiles in the lower third of your oven and remember to heat them for at least 30 minutes before you bake. The stone or tiles will even out the heat in the most cantankerous oven.

When loading the oven tiles, use a paddle made out of a piece of thin plywood. Place the loaf on the paddle with ample flour and then simply slide it onto the hot tiles. Use short jerking motions with the paddle to slide the bread off the board.

3. Be patient. Yeast takes some time to work. One of the biggest problems that people have is that they simply do not

allow the dough to rise properly, with heavy loaves the result. Calm down and enjoy the process.

4. Use fast-rising dry yeast. It will help you with your impatience with the loaf. Both Red Star and Fleischmann's make a quick, or rapid-rising, yeast, and both are excellent.

5. For the first two risings I simply put the dough on a clean countertop or cutting board and cover it with a very large stainless steel bowl. The bowl keeps the dough moist and warm and makes it easy to handle.

6. Old-fashioned cotton kitchen towels are back on the market. Use them for the final rise of your loaves. Spread out a towel on the counter and lightly flour the towel. (I use a flour sifter for this and simply tap on the side of the sifter to dust the towel with flour.) Place the loaves on the floured towel, dust them with flour on the top, and then cover the loaves with another towel. The crust will be wonderful.

7. I generally use a good-quality kitchen scale and weigh the flour. You will have much better results with bread if you are precise, and measuring cups do not always give a consistent measurement since we use them in different ways. Weighing is best. For recipes in this book that call for flour by the cup, use this method: Fill the metal measuring cup well above the top and then tap lightly on the side of the cup with a table knife. This will remove the air pockets in the flour, which result in inconsistent measuring. Level off the top of the flour with the back of the knife and proceed with the recipe.

8. Finally, I use a fine-quality electric mixer for my bread baking, though I also knead the dough a bit by hand. I like to get into it. KitchenAid makes a fine kitchen machine, and Braun makes a good one as well. I prefer the KitchenAid. Either of these machines will probably cost you less than one of those self-baking bread contraptions, and you can use the kitchen machines for a hundred other uses.

Raised Barley Loaf

Makes 2 very rich loaves

Barley is one of the oldest bread grains that we know. It was common in Egypt in very early times and it continued to be used until the development of higher forms of wheat, grains such as we know in our time. The mixing of barley and a primitive wheat, either emmer or spelt, was not uncommon in ancient times, but simple barley breads were more common.

I am proud of this recipe. My mother, a serious bread eater, can smell me baking this half a block away.

> $2^{1}/_{2}$ cups tepid water (110° to 115°)
> 2 packages fast-rising dry yeast
> 1 cup whole wheat flour
> 2 cups barley flour (available in health food stores)
> Unbleached white bread flour to make up a total weight
>   of flour of 2 pounds 3 ounces
> 2 tablespoons honey
> 2 tablespoons olive oil
> 2 teaspoons salt mixed with 2 teaspoons water

Place the water and yeast in the bowl of a heavy-duty electric mixer and stir to dissolve the yeast.

Measure out the flour as instructed. I put the whole wheat flour first, then the barley flour, into a paper lunch sack. Then I put the bag on a scale and add enough unbleached white bread flour to bring the total weight of flour to 2 pounds 3 ounces.

Put the batter blade on your mixer and slowly mix 4 cups of the flour into the yeast mixture. Allow this to form a batter and mix it until the batter pulls away from the sides of the bowl, about 10 minutes. In a glass measuring cup, combine the honey, olive oil, and the salt mixed with water. Mix into the batter until well blended.

Remove the batter blade and put the dough hook on the

machine. Slowly knead in the remaining flour until a smooth ball forms. Allow the machine to knead the dough for about 10 minutes after the dough forms a smooth ball.

(If you do not have a strong electric mixer, all of this can be done by hand. It will take a bit longer, but you will enjoy the bread. I promise.)

Remove the dough from the mixer and place it on a clean plastic countertop. Cover with a large stainless steel bowl and allow to rise until doubled in bulk, about 1 hour.

Punch down the dough, knead for just a few turns, and cover again with the bowl. Allow to rise a second time.

Preheat your oven to 450°.

When the dough has risen the second time, knead it down and form it into 2 loaves. Place a large cotton kitchen towel on the counter and dust it with flour. Place the loaves on the floured towel and dust with a bit more flour. Cover with another towel and allow to rise until doubled in bulk, about an additional 1 hour.

When ready to bake, gently turn each loaf over and place it upside down on a piece of 1/4-inch plywood. Using a very sharp small knife, cut a line about 1/4 inch deep down the center of each loaf. Slide each loaf onto hot baking tiles or an upside-down cookie sheet in preheated oven.

Bake the bread for about 35 minutes, or until the loaves are a light golden brown and offer a hollow sound when you tap them on the bottom with your finger. Cool on racks.

Unleavened Barley Cakes

Makes 12 cakes

I expect that this sort of heavy pancake affair was a great favorite among the children two thousand years ago. No, it was not a snack after Temple school, as Mother could not stop her daily cooking schedule to prepare these treats in the middle of the day. She cooked all day long, every day, always.

These cakes were probably served at any meal of the day. Since these contain no leavening of any kind, don't expect light, airy cakes but they have a delicious and sweet flavor.

This recipe is my variation on one found in *The Good Book Cookbook* (see Bibliography), a most interesting book of recipes that are based on Biblical themes and ingredients.

> **3 cups barley flour (available in health food stores)**
>
> **³/4 cup dried currants**
>
> **1¹/2 cups milk**
>
> **¹/4 teaspoon salt**
>
> **3 tablespoons honey**
>
> **Vegetable oil for panfrying**

Place the flour and currants in the bowl of a heavy-duty electric mixer.

Heat the milk in a small saucepan until hot, but do not boil or scald it. Remove from the heat and stir the salt and honey into the milk. Mix with the flour until a dough forms. It will be very sticky and heavy. (If your mixer cannot deal with this, mix the dough by hand until very smooth.)

Divide the dough into 12 balls, each a bit larger than a golf ball or about ¹/4 cup dough for each.

Oil your hands with a bit of vegetable oil (olive oil is too heavy for this dish) and flatten a ball of dough, patting it into a disk about 5 inches in diameter. Panfry in a lightly oiled, medium-hot nonstick frying pan until dark golden brown on both sides, about 4 minutes a side. Repeat with the remaining dough, adding more oil to the pan as needed.

Fine as a snack or as the bread course for any meal.

Barley Spelt Loaf

Makes 2 very rich loaves

This ancient mix of flours makes an unusual and rather sturdy loaf of bread. Barley was common, as was millet (not my favorite). However, when millet (read "birdseed") is ground into flour, it does give an interesting flavor to the bread. Spelt is simply an ancient form of wheat that is inferior to the bread wheat that we grow in our time. However, it is making a comeback with the health food crowd, and you can find it, and any of these flours, in a local health food store or wonderful left-wingy food co-op.

You'll find that this bread makes the best breakfast toast you have probably ever eaten.

2½ cups tepid water (110° to 115°)

2 packages fast-rising dry yeast

2 cups barley flour

1 cup whole wheat flour

1 cup spelt flour

1 cup millet flour

Unbleached white bread flour to make a total weight of flour of 2 pounds 3 ounces

2 tablespoons honey

2 tablespoons olive oil

2 teaspoons salt mixed with 2 teaspoons water

Place the water and the yeast in the bowl of a heavy-duty electric mixer and stir to dissolve the yeast.

Measure out the flour as instructed. I put the barley, whole wheat, spelt, and millet flours into a paper lunch sack. Then I put the bag on a scale and add enough unbleached white bread flour to bring the total weight of flour to 2 pounds 3 ounces.

Put the batter blade on your mixer and slowly mix 4 cups of the flour into the yeast mixture. Allow this to form a batter and mix it until the batter pulls away from the sides of the bowl, about 10 minutes. In a glass measuring cup, combine the honey, olive oil, and the salt mixed with water. Mix into the batter until well blended.

Remove the batter blade and put the dough hook on the machine. Slowly knead in the remaining flour until a smooth ball forms. Allow the machine to knead the dough for about 10 minutes after the dough forms a smooth ball. (If you do not have a strong electric mixer, all of this can be done by hand. It will take a bit longer, but you will enjoy the bread. I promise.)

Remove the dough from the mixer and place it on a clean plastic countertop. Cover with a large stainless steel bowl and allow to rise until doubled in bulk, about 1 hour.

Punch down the dough, knead for just a few turns, and cover again with the bowl. Allow to rise a second time.

Preheat your oven to 450°.

When the dough has risen the second time, knead it down and form it into 2 loaves. Place a large cotton kitchen towel on the counter and dust it with flour. Place the loaves on the floured towel and dust with a bit more flour. Cover with another towel and allow to rise until doubled in bulk, about an additional 1 hour.

When ready to bake, gently turn each loaf over and place it upside down on a piece of 1/4-inch plywood. Using a very sharp small knife, cut a line about 1/4 inch deep down the center of each loaf. Slide each loaf onto hot baking tiles or an upside-down cookie sheet in the preheated oven.

Bake the bread for about 35 minutes or until the loaves are a light golden brown and offer a hollow sound when you tap them on the bottom with your finger.

Four-Grain Bread
with Lentils

Makes 2 very rich loaves

"And you, take wheat and barley, beans and lentils, millet and spelt, and put them into a single vessel, and make bread of them" (Ezekiel 4:9).

There are no real recipes in the Bible, and only a few actual descriptions of dishes. The above text is certainly not a recipe but rather an admonition to the people of Israel to understand that if they are cast out of Israel, they will eat unclean foods. (No, the recipe is not unclean, but the method of baking this bread in another land would be considered unclean.) Nevertheless, I could not help wondering about how such a loaf might taste, and thus this recipe.

The reference to beans must be understood as chick-peas, or garbanzo beans, as the kind of beans that we know in our time are native to the New World and were unknown in the Old World.

All of these flours can be found in a good health food store or food co-op.

Lentils would have to be ground as flour in order to be used in bread, but I tried sprouting them for this new-old bread. The result is a loaf that is a bit heavy but very moist and just wonderful eating. Everyone will get into this one!

1/2 cup lentils, sprouted (page 134; this must be done 3 days ahead of time) and thoroughly drained

2 1/2 cups tepid water (110° to 115°)

2 packages fast-rising dry yeast

1 cup spelt flour

1 cup millet flour

1 cup barley flour

1/2 cup garbanzo (chick-pea) flour

**Unbleached white bread flour to make a total weight of
flour of 2 pounds 7 ounces**

2 tablespoons honey

2 tablespoons olive oil

2 teaspoons salt mixed with 2 teaspoons water

Sprout and drain the lentils according to the instructions on page 134. You are now ready to bake.

Place the water and yeast in the bowl of a heavy-duty electric mixer and stir to dissolve the yeast.

Measure out the flour as instructed. I put the spelt, millet, barley, and garbanzo flours into a paper lunch sack. Then I put the bag on a scale and add enough unbleached white bread flour to bring the total weight of flour to 2 pounds 7 ounces.

Put the batter blade on your mixer and slowly mix 4 cups of the flour from your total into the yeast mixture. Allow this to form a batter and mix it until the batter pulls away from the sides of the bowl, about 10 minutes. In a glass measuring cup, combine the honey, olive oil, and the salt mixed with water. Mix into the batter until well blended.

Remove the batter blade and put the dough hook on the machine. Add the thoroughly drained sprouted lentils. Slowly knead in the remaining flour until a smooth ball forms. Allow the machine to knead the dough for about 10 minutes after the dough forms a smooth ball. (If you do not have a strong electric mixer, all of this can be done by hand. It will take a bit longer, but you will enjoy the bread. I promise.)

Remove the dough from the mixer and place it on a clean plastic countertop. Cover with a large stainless steel bowl and allow to rise until doubled in bulk, about 1 hour.

Punch down the dough, knead for just a few turns, and cover again with the bowl. Allow to rise a second time.

Preheat your oven to 450°.

When the dough has risen the second time, knead it down and form it into 2 loaves. Place a large cotton kitchen towel on the counter and dust it with flour. Place the loaves on the floured towel and dust with a bit more flour. Cover with another towel and allow to rise until doubled in bulk, about 1 more hour.

continued

When ready to bake, gently turn each loaf over and place it upside down on a piece of ¼-inch plywood. Using a very sharp small knife, cut a line about ¼ inch deep down the center of each loaf. Slide each loaf onto hot baking tiles or an upside-down cookie sheet in the preheated oven.

Bake the bread for about 35 minutes, or until the loaves are a light golden brown and offer a hollow sound when you tap them on the bottom with your finger.

Sprouted Wheat Bread

Makes 2 good-sized loaves

No, I cannot find Biblical proof that such a loaf was baked during ancient times, but this is so delicious that I decided if they did not bake it, they should have! All of the ingredients were available, and I am sure that someone must have tried this.

This kind of bread is very popular with the health food store crowd, and I think you will enjoy it as well. Do not bother trying to sprout emmer wheat or spelt. It does not work half as well as whole wheat or wheat berries.

½ cup wheat berries (page 101), sprouted (page 134, this will take 2 to 3 days; see Note)

2¾ cups tepid water (110° to 115°)

2 packages fast-rising dry yeast

2 cups whole wheat flour

Unbleached white bread flour to make a total weight of flour of 2 pounds 3 ounces

1 teaspoon salt mixed with 1 tablespoon water

Sprout the wheatberries according to instructions on page 134.

Place the water and yeast in the bowl of a heavy-duty electric mixer and stir to dissolve the yeast.

Measure out the flour as instructed. I put the whole wheat flour in a paper lunch sack. Then I put the bag on a scale and add enough unbleached white bread flour to bring the total weight of flour to 2 pounds 3 ounces.

Using the batter blade, slowly mix 4 cups of the flour into the yeast mixture. Mix until the batter begins to pull away from the sides of the mixing bowl, about 10 minutes. Add the salt mixed with water to the batter. Mix in the sprouted wheat and the remaining flour. I use a dough hook for this. Knead until the dough pulls away from the sides of the bowl, about 15 minutes. (If you do not have a strong electric mixer, all of this can be done by hand.)

Remove the dough from the bowl and place on a clean plastic countertop. Cover with a large stainless steel bowl and allow to rise until doubled in bulk, about 1 hour.

Punch down the dough, knead for a moment, and cover with the bowl again. Allow to rise again until doubled in bulk.

Punch down the dough and shape into 2 large loaves. Place on a floured cotton kitchen towel. Flour the top of the loaves and cover with another cotton kitchen towel. Allow to rise until doubled in bulk, about 2 hours for this heavy loaf.

Turn the loaves over and cut a very thin slash in the top of each loaf. Use a razor blade for this or a very sharp knife. Bake on a sheet pan sprinkled with a bit of cornmeal or on a preheated pizza brick or oven stone. Bake at 375° to 400° until the bottoms of the loaves are firm and sound hollow when you tap them.

Remove from the oven and cool on racks. (This will preserve the crunchy crust.)

NOTE: Do not let the wheat berries sprout longer than 2 or 3 days, as the green part of the sprouts will become too long and a tad bitter.

Sesame Bread

Makes 2 loaves (and wonderful toast)

Sesame seed, associated in our culture with foods from the Orient, was common in Biblical times. I love the flavor and use sesame oil in many dishes. This is a mild and tasty loaf.

Buy the sesame oil in an Asian market, and purchase the sesame seeds there as well. Your supermarket will charge you too much for sesame seeds.

1 batch Raised Barley Loaf (page 179), prepared to the batter stage

2 tablespoons toasted sesame oil

7 tablespoons raw sesame seeds

Prepare the Raised Barley Loaf dough to the batter stage; stir in the sesame oil and 3 tablespoons of the sesame seeds. Continue with the loaf recipe, adding the remaining flours.

When the loaves are risen and you are about to bake, brush each loaf with a bit of water and top each with 2 tablespoons of the sesame seeds. Bake as directed.

Fennel Bread

Makes 2 very tasty loaves

Fennel is an ancient spice as well as a vegetable. The seeds were used in many dishes, and this variation on an old theme is unusually good. The idea of putting spice seeds in bread is actually Greek, but the method moved into Egypt in very early times.

Fennel seeds taste a bit like licorice or anise and are of the same family.

1 batch Raised Barley Loaf (page 179), prepared to the batter stage

1 tablespoon freshly ground fennel seed (I grind mine in a small electric coffee grinder), plus 1 tablespoon whole fennel seeds

2 tablespoons milk

Prepare the Raised Barley Loaf dough to the batter stage. Stir in the ground fennel and finish the dough by adding the remaining flours. Allow the loaves to rise.

Just before baking, brush the tops of the loaves with the milk and sprinkle with the whole fennel seeds. Bake as directed.

Desert Flat Bread
(Pita or Pocket Bread)

Makes 12 loaves, enough for a dinner party of 8 to 10

This is one of the oldest breads that we know of in the Bible. When the Children of Israel went south into Egypt looking for the promised bread grains, they brought with them the sourdough, or yeast, they had had for many generations. This recipe is very close to what they did with that leavening.

My Uncle Vic Abdo taught me to make this bread. His parents came from Syria, and when I was a child he would feed me this loaf and exclaim, "Moses baked this on the desert!" So I grew up thinking that Moses was Syrian. Then, at the end of World War II the borders in the Middle East were changed around, and my dear uncle declared that he was no longer Syrian but Lebanese. So, Moses became Lebanese. It took me a while to straighten all of this out, but the bread recipe remained the same. Good things do not change.

No, for the millionth time, I am not Lebanese but Norwegian. My mother's sister married this gorgeous Lebanese gentleman, and thus I have a Lebanese uncle.

This bread is most often called pita bread or pocket bread in this country. It serves as the main bread in much of the Middle East and it is used as the eating implement in many lands. Silverware is not used—only the bread as an eating tool—and thus all meals become a sort of wonderful sandwich.

> 2 cups tepid water (110° to 115°)
>
> 2 packages fast-rising dry yeast
>
> 5 cups unbleached white bread flour
>
> 1 cup whole wheat flour
>
> 1 teaspoon salt mixed with 1 teaspoon water

Place the water and yeast in the bowl of a heavy-duty electric mixer and stir to dissolve the yeast. Measure out the flour. The 6 cups of flour will weigh about 1 pound 15 ounces.

Put the batter blade on your electric mixer and mix in 4 cups of the total flour. Beat this until the batter is smooth and begins to pull away from the sides of the bowl, about 10 minutes. Add the salt mixed with water.

Replace the batter blade with the dough hook and knead in the rest of the flour. Continue to knead until the dough is very smooth and no longer sticks to the sides of the mixing bowl.

Remove the dough from the mixing bowl and place it on a clean plastic countertop. Cover it with a large stainless steel bowl and allow it to rise until doubled in bulk, about 1 hour.

Punch down the dough and allow it to rise a second time. At the end of the second rising, punch down the dough, knead it for a moment, and then divide the dough into 12 equal-size balls. Place each on cotton kitchen towels that have been dusted with flour. Sprinkle just a little flour on the top of each ball, and cover with another cotton kitchen towel. Allow the balls to rise until doubled in bulk, about an additional 1 hour.

Meanwhile, turn your oven to the highest possible temperature: Place the thermostat on Broil and the heating elements on Bake. If you are going to bake on oven bricks, be sure they are in the oven when you begin the preheating. If you are going to bake on a cookie sheet or baking sheet, place it upside down in the oven.

Now we are ready to bake. If you have an oven with a glass door, be sure to call the kids, as each loaf will blow up like a ball during baking.

Lightly flour the plastic countertop and punch down the first ball, being careful not to put fingernail holes in the surface of the dough; just flatten it with your hand. Using ample flour, roll out the circle of dough until it is 8 to 9 inches in diameter. Place the loaf on a piece of 1/4-inch plywood. Using a quick jerking motion, slide it onto the hot bricks or upside-down cookie sheet in the preheated oven. Do not leave the door open for more than a few seconds, as the oven must be hot enough to cause the loaf to puff up almost immediately.

Watch through the glass door until the expanded loaf takes on a few light brown spots. This will take only a few minutes. Remove the loaf from the hot brick or sheet and place it on a heavy kitchen towel. Cover it with another heavy kitchen towel so that as it cools, the steam inside the loaf will be absorbed by the bread itself. Continue with the next loaf, placing each loaf on top of the previous one and covering it with the heavy towel.

NOTE: If you do not have success with the first loaf, do not despair. I can seldom get the first one to rise myself. Simply be careful in the rolling of the dough, since a wrinkle or tear will allow the steam to escape rather than to raise the loaf. You may also be rolling them too thin.

After baking all of the loaves, seal them in a plastic bag for storage at room temperature until eaten, or for longer storage in the refrigerator. These are best eaten on the day they are baked.

Pita Bread with Za'atar

This is very simple and just delicious. My Lebanese Uncle Vic serves this as people have cocktails just before dinner. Za'atar is a mixture of sumac, hyssop, thyme, and sesame seeds, and it is a common spice blend in the street markets of the Middle East. You can find it in Middle Eastern markets in any large city in America.

Prepare the loaves as for Pita with Hyssop and Sumac (page 193), but use za'atar (page 101) instead of the hyssop, sumac, and sesame seeds.

This is a favorite in our family. You can even cheat and use pita bread from the market. Just brush it with olive oil and top it with za'atar. Place it under a hot broiler for a few moments and you are set!

Pita with Hyssop
and Sumac

This is an ancient way of preparing bread so that it can become a meal in itself. All you need is a glass of wine and you are ready for a good meal.

You can buy dried hyssop in spice shops or Middle Eastern shops throughout the country. This Biblical herb is blended with sumac and sesame seeds to create a very rich topping for the flat bread. Doesn't this predate the pizza?

You need not bake the entire batch of pita dough in this manner. Why not cook a couple of loaves with the topping and leave the rest plain? You are prepared for the whole meal.

Desert Flat Bread (Pita) (page 190), ready to bake

Olive oil

Dried hyssop (page 99)

Sumac (page 101)

Raw sesame seeds

Prepare a batch of Desert Flat Bread. Roll out and prepare it for baking. Just before you slide each pita into the hot oven, poke the circle of dough about 15 times with a fork all around the loaf. Brush with a bit of olive oil and sprinkle with hyssop, sumac, and sesame seeds. Slide into the hot oven and bake as directed.

The loaf will not rise since you poked holes in the dough. However, you will have a lovely loaf that works very well as a first course before dinner from Biblical times.

Coarse Wheat Bread

Makes 2 very rich loaves

This bread is simple to make and absolutely delicious. It has great flavors from the ancient world and I claim that it is simple because you need not mold the loaves. You can use (gasp!) bread pans. For this kind of bread, pans work very well. The use of bulgur wheat offers a bit of dense flavor that I find delightful.

> 1 cup fine-ground bulgur wheat (page 98) soaked in 1 quart of water for 30 minutes, then drained very well in a strainer
>
> 2½ cups tepid water (110° to 115°)
>
> 2 packages fast-rising dry yeast
>
> 2 cups whole wheat flour
>
> Unbleached white bread flour to make a total weight of flour of 2 pounds 3 ounces
>
> 2 tablespoons honey
>
> 2 tablespoons olive oil
>
> 2 teaspoons salt mixed with 2 teaspoons water

Soak the bulgur wheat in 1 quart of water for 30 minutes. Drain very well.

Place the water and yeast in the bowl of heavy-duty electric mixer and stir to dissolve the yeast.

Measure out the flour as instructed. I put the whole wheat flour in a paper lunch sack. Then I put the bag on a scale and add enough unbleached white bread flour to bring the total weight of flour to 2 pounds 3 ounces.

Put the batter blade on your mixer and slowly mix 4 cups of the flour into the yeast mixture. Allow this to form a batter and mix it until the batter pulls away from the sides of the bowl, about 10 minutes. In a glass measuring cup, combine the honey, olive oil, and the salt mixed with water. Mix into the batter until well blended.

Remove the batter blade and put the dough hook on the machine. Add the soaked and *well-drained* bulgur wheat. Slowly knead in the remaining flour until a smooth ball forms. Allow the machine to knead the dough for about 10 minutes after the dough forms a smooth ball. (If you do not have a strong electric mixer, all of this can be done by hand. It will take a bit longer, but you will enjoy the bread. I promise.)

Remove the dough from the mixer and place it in a large stainless steel bowl. The dough will be rather moist, but don't worry about it. Cover it with a towel and allow it to rise until doubled in bulk, about 1 hour.

Stir it down and allow it to rise again.

Preheat your oven to 375°.

Using olive oil, grease 2 nonstick bread baking pans (each 9 by 5 inches and 2½ inches deep). Divide the dough between the two pans and allow the loaves to rise another hour.

Bake the loaves in a preheated oven for about 40 minutes, until golden brown.

Coarse Wheat Bread with Garlic

Makes 2 loaves for garlic lovers

No, I cannot prove that such a loaf was common in Biblical times, but no matter. This is really good and any garlic fan will love it.

1 batch Coarse Wheat Bread (page 194), prepared to the batter stage

4 large cloves garlic, crushed

Prepare a batch of Coarse Wheat Bread to the batter stage. Stir in the garlic and continue in completing the recipe (page 194).

Bake as directed, and watch the neighbors sniff the air!

Semolina Bread

Makes 2 very rich loaves

I suppose I should not be giving you this recipe in this book since it uses a flour that was not available in ancient times. However, I just discovered this bread and I developed the recipe based on a wonderful loaf available at Claudio's Cheese and Olives in Philadelphia. When I shared it with Craig, our chef, he said, "It is too good not to put in the book. Hey, we owe our readers!" He's right, as he always is. Therefore, a loaf that's a joy to make and a blessing to eat. I guess that's as Biblical as it gets.

2½ cups tepid water (110° to 115°)

2 packages fast-rising dry yeast

1 cup semolina flour (find in Italian delicatessens)

Unbleached white bread flour to make a total weight of
    flour of 2 pounds 8 ounces

3 large eggs, beaten

2 tablespoons butter, melted and cooled

1 tablespoon sugar

2 teaspoons salt mixed with 2 teaspoons water

¼ cup sesame seeds for topping

Place the water and yeast in the bowl of a heavy-duty electric mixer and stir to dissolve the yeast.

Measure out the flour as instructed. I put the semolina flour in a paper lunch sack. Then I put the bag on a scale and add enough unbleached white bread flour to bring the total weight of flour to 2 pounds 8 ounces.

Put the batter blade on your mixer and slowly mix 4 cups of the flour into the yeast mixture. Allow this to form a batter and mix it until the batter pulls away from the sides of the bowl, about 10 minutes. In a glass measuring cup, combine the eggs, melted butter, sugar, and the salt mixed with water. Mix into the batter until well blended.

continued

Remove the batter blade and put the dough hook on the machine. Slowly knead in the remaining flour until a smooth ball forms. Allow the machine to knead the dough for about 10 minutes after the dough forms a smooth ball. (If you do not have a strong electric mixer, all of this can be done by hand. It will take a bit longer, but you will enjoy the bread. I promise.)

Remove the dough from the mixer and place it on a clean plastic countertop. Cover with a large stainless steel bowl and allow to rise until doubled in bulk, about 1 hour.

Punch down the dough, knead for just a few turns, and cover again with the bowl. Allow to rise a second time.

Preheat your oven to 450°.

When the dough has risen the second time, knead it down and form it into 2 loaves. Place a large cotton kitchen towel on the counter and dust it with flour. Place the loaves on the floured towel and dust with a bit more flour. Cover with another towel and allow to rise until doubled in bulk, about an additional 1 hour.

When ready to bake, gently turn each loaf over and place it upside down on a piece of 1/4-inch plywood. Brush the tops of the loaves with a bit of water and top with the sesame seeds. Using a very sharp small knife, cut a line about 1/4 inch deep down the center of each loaf. Slide each loaf onto hot baking tiles or an upside-down cookie sheet in a preheated oven.

Bake the bread for about 35 minutes, or until the loaves are a light golden brown and offer a hollow sound when you tap them on the bottom with your finger.

Yogurt-Raised Wheat Bread

Makes 2 unusual and very delicious loaves

Leavening for bread in the ancient world was probably similar to what we call sourdough. Wild yeast spores floating in the air could easily infect the leavening, causing it to become "sour" and "unclean." The same was true of cheese and yogurt products.

When I prepared a batch of Kishk (page 216), I noted the amount of gas and airiness the yogurt produced, very much like yeast or sourdough. I produced this recipe on a lark, and it turned out to be one of the best loaves of bread I have ever eaten. It is just a tiny bit sour and yet sweet at the same time. It is easy to prepare, but you must allow the dough to ferment for about five days. Don't worry, you do little work during the five days.

This would be fun to try and fun to show to the kids. They will get a kick out of watching the dough rise and bubble a bit.

Use the recipe for Coarse Wheat Bread (page 194) with the following changes: Reduce the water to 2 cups and substitute 1 cup Homemade Yogurt (page 204) for the yeast.

Instead of mixing the water and dry yeast mentioned in the above recipe, mix the water and yogurt in the bowl of a heavy-duty electric mixer. Add the remaining ingredients and finish the dough as instructed.

When the moist dough is completed, place it in a stainless steel bowl or a ceramic crock large enough to allow the dough to double in bulk. Cover with a towel and place in a cool place, perhaps the basement. (Do not refrigerate, or the process will take many more days and the dough will probably sour.) Allow the dough to ferment for 5 days, stirring it down every other day.

When you are ready to bake, turn your oven to 375° and follow the baking instructions for Coarse Wheat Bread.

Desert Cheese

No, that is not "dessert cheese" but rather "desert cheese." It seems that cheese was actually discovered in the desert. Note I did not say "invented," as Biblical peoples would never claim to have invented such a thing. Rather, they give thanks for the fact that the Holy One gave them cheese.

How did it come about? Well, in nomadic communities milk was often kept in bags made from goat stomachs. Given the heat from the desert and the natural rennet that was in the goat stomachs, curds were formed, and hence the discovery of cheese. It is true that most of our great discoveries in the food world came about by accident. We can hardly claim to be the creators or inventors.

A second way that cheese was made in the desert came about when they were simply trying to save milk. It became infected, no, blessed by a wild strain of yeast that seems to be common in the desert, and yogurt was formed. Yogurt will keep for days, even in the desert, and cheese can be made from yogurt, of course.

I want you to make your own yogurt. It is so easy and it is far superior to that stuff from the market. Further, it will cost about a quarter of the price of the grocery version, so it is frugal, fresh, and perfect for your desert cooking.

Homemade Yogurt

Makes 4 quarts

This is an ancient way of preserving milk, and from it comes a long list of wonderful other blessings, everything from the yogurt itself to cheese and cooking sauces. All of these were common to desert life.

I am sure that one reason that most people don't make their own yogurt is that they think they do not have time. Actually, it is a simple process that takes very little time.

A second reason that people are slow to make their own yogurt is the belief that you must have lot of special electric gadgets and equipment. Not so. You will pay for your cheese thermometer on your first try at making yogurt. Everything else you need for this recipe is already in your home. So relax, and make a product that is far superior to the stuff from the market. It is also much less expensive than the market product.

6- to 8-quart stainless steel or enamel pot

Heat diffuser or flame tamer

**Cheese or yeast thermometer (needs to register from 100°
to 220°; find in gourmet shops)**

Electric heating pad

4 1-quart wide-mouth canning jars with lids

INGREDIENTS

4 quarts fresh whole milk, skim milk, or low-fat milk

**2 5-gram packages Bulgarian or other yogurt starter
(find in health food stores)**

Pour the milk into the stainless steel pot, place your heat diffuser on the burner, and slowly heat the milk to 180°, checking
carefully with your cheese thermometer. You do not want to
overheat it. Stir regularly with a stainless steel spoon. Remove
from the heat and cool to 115°.

Set the heating pad at Low.

Place 2 cups of the hot milk in a clean glass measuring cup
and stir in the yogurt starter until thoroughly dissolved; then stir
the mixture into the pot of warm milk. Divide this among the
canning jars and seal each one.

Place the jars in a pot of warm water (115°); the water
should come about halfway up the sides of the jars. Cover the
pot and place the pot on the warm heating pad. Wrap the whole
pot with a large bath towel, and sit down and relax. Eight hours
later you will have fine yogurt. If you want to make this in the
evening, leave it to sit overnight. The yogurt will have even more
flavor. Refrigerate the yogurt before using.

When you are ready to make more yogurt, use the same
recipe but use only 3½ quarts of milk. Stir 2 cups of your old
batch of yogurt into the tepid milk instead of the packaged
starter. You can do this for several batches.

Yogurt Cheese

Makes about 5 cups

This is a great product for those of us who are trying to cut down on fat—but not on flavor. Certainly it must have been a common method of cheese making in the ancient world, and many Middle Eastern cultures still make this cheese in the same way.

This cheese has a slightly tart or sour, but very fresh, flavor. It is great on toast and fine in cooking.

Of course you do not need to use a gallon of yogurt for a bit of this cheese. Make any amount you wish!

1 batch Homemade Yogurt (page 204)

Place a piece of cheesecloth or muslin (2 feet by 2 feet) in a large colander. Place the colander in a large bowl or sink and add the yogurt. Bring up the corners of the cloth and tie them together. Hang this bag over the bowl and let drain overnight.

By the next day, you will have a product that is very close to cream cheese in texture, but not in butterfat content. Cream cheese is 32 percent butterfat; yogurt cheese contains a tenth of that amount.

Yogurt Cheese with Herbs

Makes about 2½ cups

This will probably remind you of one of those expensive soft herb cheeses from France . . . but all of these ingredients are from Biblical times. Shall we have a cocktail party for those Roman soldiers?

2½ cups Yogurt Cheese (page 206)

2 tablespoons chopped fresh dill

3 cloves garlic, crushed

1 tablespoon chopped fresh mint

1½ tablespoons chopped fresh thyme

Salt and freshly ground black pepper to taste

Combine all the ingredients in a stainless steel bowl and stir until smooth. Refrigerate overnight in a covered plastic refrigerator carton.

Use as a spread on bread, toast rounds, or crackers. You may want to broil these for a nice snack.

VARIATION: Substitute 2½ tablespoons chopped fresh hyssop (page 99) for the mint and thyme.

Sautéed Onions with Yogurt

Serves 6 as a side dish or many more as an appetizer dip

I offer this dish to get you into thinking about using yogurt instead of heavy cream sauces. You can use yogurt on everything from potato salad to fish. And the flavor is bright and fresh. Yes, I know this makes a large amount. But then you can cut it down and make any amount you wish.

2 tablespoons olive oil

1 clove garlic, thinly sliced

10 cups thinly sliced yellow onions

1 tablespoon dried hyssop (page 99) or 1 teaspoon dried thyme

2 teaspoons caraway seed

2 tablespoons chopped fresh parsley

2 cups Homemade Yogurt (page 204)

Salt and freshly ground black pepper to taste

Pita Bread (page 190) for serving

Heat a large frying pan or Dutch oven and add the oil, garlic, and onions (you may have to do this in a couple of batches). Sauté over medium heat for 3 minutes. Add the hyssop, caraway, and parsley and toss together. Reduce the heat to low and cover the pan. Allow the onion mixture to sweat down until tender, for 5 to 10 minutes, stirring occasionally. Stir in the yogurt and add salt and pepper to taste. Heat until the yogurt is warm, but don't boil. Serve with cut pieces of pita bread.

Red Meat on the
Biblical Table

We have all these romanticized versions of shepherd boys sitting around the evening fire roasting lamb for their supper. Not a likely scene. Lamb was very expensive. Sheep were the providers of milk, of wool, of cheese—in short, meat was the last thing that the lamb was expected to offer. A young lamb would be roasted during the High Holy Days, but for the rest of the year, the diet was rather bland.

Cattle were sometimes eaten. The kings and rulers did have enormous feasts, serving goats, fatted calves, and oxen, but these were not meals to which the common person was invited. It is true that the animals that were sacrificed at the temple altar could then be eaten, but we are talking real expense and rarity here.

There are wonderful Biblical references to the earliest times in which everything was in harmony among all creatures. Thus, in the Garden of Eden, God gave us food, "every plant yielding seed which is upon the face of the earth, and every tree with seed in its fruit" (Genesis 1:29). This is a reference to the perfect world in the Garden of Eden, but following the Great Flood, man and woman were permitted to eat meat. Even then, however, blood was not to be consumed, since it is a symbol of life.

What do we do with the argument between the meat eaters and the vegetarians? We have eaten meat from the beginning and that seems to be the diet for which we are suited. In those ancient days, the consumption of a fatted calf was allowed if a special guest came to one's home. Witness Abraham cooking a meal for the angels and the Prodigal Son being welcomed home by his father with a fatted calf. In Biblical lands, red meat was either roasted or boiled, but the Pascal Lamb was always roasted. In Rome, on the other hand, roasted meat was thought to be inferior to boiled meat. The Romans seemed to boil almost everything.

Meat or no, it is plain that in our time we have wandered very far from the limited meat diet of those early days. We eat too much meat, that's all there is to it. Although we must increase our consumption of fruits and vegetables, grains, and legumes, it seems to me that a little meat is necessary to our diet.

The recipes in this chapter are all easy to prepare and few require anything that might be called unusual. Further, since most of them are stews, they are to be eaten with grains, so we actually are cutting down on our red meat intake and increasing our grain intake . . . and the flavors that result are delicious.

Barley with Lamb

Serves 6

This is a very rich, thick, and tasty dish, one of my favorites in this collection. One pound of lamb feeds six people, not an easy stunt, but you will be very satisfied by the deep flavors and the tastes of the ancient world.

> 2 tablespoons butter
>
> 1 cup barley, rinsed and drained
>
> 2 tablespoons olive oil
>
> 3 cloves garlic, crushed
>
> 2 medium yellow onions, peeled and chopped
>
> 1 pound boneless lamb stewing meat, trimmed of excess fat
>
> Salt and freshly ground black pepper to taste
>
> 6 cups Chicken Stock (page 118)

Melt the butter in a 4-quart stove-top casserole and brown the barley for 2 to 3 minutes. Remove from the heat.

Heat a large frying pan and add 1 tablespoon of the oil. Add the garlic and onions, and sauté for 5 minutes. Add to the barley.

Season the lamb with salt and pepper to taste. Heat the frying pan again and add the remaining 1 tablespoon oil. Brown the lamb and add to the casserole. Add 3 cups of the stock, cover and bake in a preheated 350° oven for 1 hour or until the liquid is almost absorbed.

Add the remaining 3 cups stock, cover, and bake for 50 minutes more, or until the meat is tender. Add salt and pepper to taste.

Baked Kibbeh

Serves 6 to 8

This dish offers several stories, so hang on. I first tasted this dish when I was a tiny child. My Uncle Vic, who is Lebanese, married into our Norwegian family, and he brought some real excitement to our food. He eats kibbeh raw with pita bread, as is the custom in the land of his parents. Of course Jews would never eat raw meat, so I have given you the baked version. It is certainly delicious enough, but it is not the Middle Eastern version of steak tartare.

In early times, raw grain was roasted and then chopped and cooked. It was the ancestor of bulgur wheat, an invention of the desert. It was called "parched grain" or "crushed grain."

In the book of Proverbs, the Fool and the Wise Man are discussed constantly. The Wise Man knows and relies upon the Law or Word of God, and the Fool is the one who just cannot seem to catch on. The author of Proverbs writes in Hebrew and therefore uses very graphic images. Wonderful! The author claims that the Fool is so far from understanding his responsibility to the true nature of Judaism that one could "crush a fool in a mortar with a pestle along with crushed grain, yet his folly will not depart from him" (Proverbs 27:22). Isn't this kibbeh? What a fate for the poor Fool (an imaginary fate, of course).

This is one of my favorite lamb dishes. It is grand when hot, eaten with pita bread; it's great cold with yogurt; and it makes an incredible sandwich in the middle of the night when everyone else is asleep. Yes, I do that often.

1 cup fine-ground bulgur wheat

3 cups cold water

2 pounds boneless lean leg of lamb, trimmed of all fat and
  gristle

3/4 cup chopped yellow onion

1 1/2 tablespoons chopped fresh mint

2 cloves garlic, chopped

$^1\!/_2$ teaspoon ground cinnamon

$^1\!/_2$ teaspoon ground cumin

2 teaspoons salt

2 tablespoons olive oil

2 tablespoons coarsely chopped skinned pistachios

Place the bulgur wheat in a small bowl and add 3 cups cold water. Allow to soak for 1 hour. Drain well.

Grind the lamb through your coarsest meat grinder blade into a large bowl. Add the bulgur, onion, mint, garlic, cinnamon, cumin, and salt. Mix well with a wooden spoon. Then grind the mixture again, using the fine blade.

Grease a 10-inch round cake pan with 1 tablespoon of the oil. Add the meat mixture and smooth it out in the pan. Using a sharp paring knife, score the top of the meat in a diamond pattern. Sprinkle the top with the chopped pistachios and drizzle with the remaining 1 tablespoon oil. Bake in a preheated 375° oven for 35 to 45 minutes, until the kibbeh is firm and cooked throughout but not dry. Cut into wedges and serve.

Kishk

Makes 8½ cups (2½ pounds);
this will give your family 6 to 8 wonderful meals

I think this dish is a real wonder of the ancient world. Yogurt is mixed with bulgur wheat to make a thick mush. This is allowed to ferment for a few days and then spread on a sheet to dry in the sun. Finally, it is ground into flour and stored for a few months before use in the winter months.

This yogurty-wheaty smelling dish is absolutely delicious. My Lebanese Uncle Vic made this for me when I was a child, and I make it to this day. But I warn you that this will take a few months to make, so don't call someone and invite them over for dinner tomorrow. The fact that it takes months to prepare should help us to understand the intense laboring that went into preparing food in the ancient world.

You can buy this mixture already prepared in Middle Eastern shops, but it will be much older than your homemade and have a much more sour or stale flavor.

THE MAKING OF THE KISHK FLOUR

2 pounds coarse-ground bulgur wheat

3 quarts Homemade Yogurt (page 204)

Place the bulgur in a 6- to 8-quart crock and stir in 2 quarts of the yogurt. Cover the crock with cheesecloth and seal with a large rubber band placed around the rim of the crock. Place in a cool spot.

On the second day stir in 3 more cups of yogurt and seal the cheesecloth. Place in a cool spot. On the third day, stir in the last cup of yogurt and seal. The mixture should be thick and moist.

Let the mixture sit in a cool place for about 7 more days, stirring the mixture thoroughly once each day. Using a clean rubber spatula, scrape down the sides of the crock each time after you stir so as to prevent small pieces of grain from clinging to the side of the crock, drying out, and spoiling.

At the end of the 10 days, the crock will have a wonderful perfume of cheese and wheat, which is exactly what you want.

In the ancient world you would now spread this out on a sheet and dry it in the sun. Perhaps you can do this in California, but not in Seattle. In Seattle I simply spread the mixture out on a plastic countertop to about ½ inch thick. I then turn a fan on it and let it dry. TWICE A DAY, BE SURE TO ROLL THE MIXTURE BETWEEN YOUR PALMS SO THAT THE GRAINS BEGIN TO SEPA-RATE. As they dry, eventually any clumps will fall apart into individual grains. The drying will take about 6 more days.

When the grains are completely dry and each grain is separated, grind the grains medium-fine in a flour grinder or food processor, as for whole wheat flour. If you use a food processor, you will need to pass the flour through a flour sifter after grinding and regrind the remaining coarse grains.

Place the flour in a cotton kitchen towel bag (you will have to make this by sewing up a cotton kitchen towel). Hang it in a cool place to continue to dry for about 10 days or so. Then place it in a large glass jar, seal tightly, and store in a cool, dark place for another 2 months before use.

THE COOKING OF KISHK AND LAMB
1 quart cooked Kishk serves 4

Now, if you are with me after all of the above, we are ready to cook a typical desert dinner. When you cut up the lamb, leave a little fat on the meat for flavor.

2 tablespoons olive oil

½ pound boneless lamb shoulder, cut into ¼-inch-thick julienne strips

3 large cloves garlic, crushed

1 cup Kishk

4 cups cold water

Heat the olive oil in a heavy-bottomed 3-quart pot and add the lamb. Sauté over medium heat for a few minutes until brown. Add the garlic and cook until the garlic is tender. Stir in the kishk, and continue to stir until the flour has absorbed all the juices and lamb fat and there are no lumps. Move off the heat and stir in the cold water. Return to the burner and bring to a simmer, stirring often. Simmer gently, stirring often, for about 20 minutes, uncovered, until the kishk thickens to the consistency of a light pudding or light Cream of Wheat.

GARNISHES

Cucumber slices

Greek olives

Green onions

Romaine lettuce leaves

Pita Bread (page 190), cut into quarters

To serve, place about a cup of the lamb kishk on each warm large dinner plate. Surround the kishk with all of the garnishes, and dip them into the wonderful pudding to eat.

I know this looks as if it takes Eternity to make, but it is Heaven to eat!

Lamb Stew with Figs and Wine

Serves 4 to 6

This is a variation of a recipe we found in an interesting volume called *The Good Book Cookbook* (see Bibliography). It offers recipes that make good use of foods that were common in Biblical times but are, I think, very up to date. This is a delicious dish and I urge you to try it.

> 3 pounds boneless lamb stewing meat, trimmed of excess fat
>
> Salt and freshly ground black pepper to taste
>
> 2 tablespoons olive oil
>
> 2 cloves garlic, crushed
>
> 1 1/2 cups dry red wine
>
> 1/2 cup water
>
> 2 teaspoons dry mustard
>
> 2 teaspoons ground coriander
>
> 2 teaspoons ground cumin
>
> 1 cup dried figs, halved

Season the meat with salt and pepper to taste. Heat a large frying pan and add 1 tablespoon of the oil. Brown half of the lamb and remove it to a 4- to 6-quart pot. Brown the remaining lamb in the same manner, using another tablespoon of oil.

Add the remaining ingredients to the pot. Bring to a boil, cover, and simmer gently, stirring occasionally, for 1 1/2 hours, or until the lamb is very tender. Add salt and pepper to taste.

Lamb Stew with Fruits and Cinnamon

Serves 4 to 6

In this country we usually do not combine fruit with meat. But in the ancient world, this was a common practice, and for very good reason. It gave richness to the dish, added wonderful sweet flavors, and stretched the meat contained in the dish. Meat was used as a flavoring in the ancient world, not as the center of the meal. We have much to learn from these old-style recipes.

We have substituted an apple for the quince that would have been used in this dish. After all, apples as we know them came from this country and were not known in the ancient world. What the Bible refers to as an "apple" is really a quince.

3 pounds boneless lamb stewing meat, trimmed of
    excess fat

Salt and freshly ground black pepper to taste

2 tablespoons olive oil

1 medium yellow onion, peeled and diced

1½ cups Chicken Stock (page 118)

1 large Red Delicious apple, cored and coarsely chopped

½ cup golden raisins

1½-inch piece cinnamon stick

1 tablespoon pomegranate molasses (available in Middle
    Eastern markets)

1 tablespoon chopped fresh parsley

Season the lamb with salt and pepper to taste. Heat a large frying pan and add 1 tablespoon of the oil. Brown half the meat and remove it to a 4- to 6-quart pot. Brown the remaining lamb, using the remaining 1 tablespoon oil.

Add the onion and chicken stock to the pot. Bring to a boil, cover, and simmer for 1 hour.

Add the remaining ingredients and simmer, covered, for 30 to 45 minutes more, until the lamb is very tender. Remove the cinnamon stick. Add salt and pepper to taste.

Lamb and Lentil Stew

Serves 6

So old, this dish is so old. Lentils are one of the oldest legumes that we know of, and they were certainly common throughout the Middle East thousands of years ago. They are also the most nutritious legume in our diet. Your family will love this dish.

3 pounds boneless lamb stewing meat, trimmed of excess fat

Salt and freshly ground black pepper to taste

3 tablespoons olive oil

3 cloves garlic, chopped

1 large yellow onion, peeled and thinly sliced

1/2 cup dry white wine

4 cups Chicken Stock (page 118)

1/4 cup chopped fresh parsley

1 cup lentils

Season the lamb with salt and pepper to taste. Heat a large frying pan and add 1 tablespoon of the oil. Brown half of the lamb and remove it to a 4- to 6-quart pot. Brown the remaining lamb in the same manner, using another tablespoon of oil.

Heat the pan again and add the remaining 1 tablespoon oil. Add the garlic and onion and sauté until tender. Add to the pot. Deglaze the frying pan with the wine, scraping up the pan brownings as they dissolve in the wine. Add to the pot along with 2 cups of the chicken stock. Bring to a simmer and simmer, covered, for 1½ hours.

Add the parsley, lentils, and remaining 2 cups stock and simmer gently, covered, for 45 minutes more, or until lentils are tender. Add salt and pepper to taste.

Lamb Chops with Fennel Seed

Serves 4

Fennel gives lamb a most interesting flavor. Please do not overcook these chops. One of the bad memories of our days in grade
school was overcooked lamb. Don't do that in our time, please.

> 8 thick-cut lamb loin chops (about 3 to 4 ounces each),
>   trimmed of excess fat
>
> 3 cloves garlic, crushed
>
> Salt and freshly ground black pepper to taste
>
> 1½ teaspoons fennel seed
>
> 1 tablespoon olive oil
>
> ½ cup dry red wine

Season the lamb chops with the garlic and salt and pepper to
taste. Press the fennel seed into the chops on both sides.

Heat a large nonstick frying pan and add the oil. Add the
seasoned lamb chops in two batches and brown on both sides.
Add the wine, cover, reduce the heat, and simmer gently for
about 5 minutes, turning once. Serve the chops with the juices
that have formed in the pan.

Lamb Chops Grilled with Sumac

Serves 4

I must warn you about the use of sumac in your kitchen. Once you begin using it, you are going to find yourself putting it on everything from rice to chicken. It is a wonderful gift from the ancient world.

8 thick-cut lamb loin chops (about 3 to 4 ounces each), trimmed of excess fat

2 tablespoons sumac (page 101)

Salt and freshly ground black pepper to taste

Juice of 2 lemons

Olive oil for brushing

Season the meat on both sides with the sumac and salt and pepper to taste. Rub with the lemon juice and allow to marinate for 45 minutes.

Prepare a hot fire in a grill. Brush the lamb chops with olive oil and grill over high heat for 3 minutes per side for medium-rare. Drizzle with the remaining lemon juice and serve.

Grilled Lamb Chops
with Garlic in Grape Leaves

Serves 4

Nothing was wasted in the ancient world. Food was so scarce that they even took to eating the leaves off the grapevines. We have all tasted stuffed grape leaves, but cooking meat wrapped in them is a wonderful delight. It is now a very "in" practice among the Mediterranean eating crowd.

> 8 lamb rib chops (about 3 to 4 ounces each)
> Salt and freshly ground black pepper to taste
> 3 cloves garlic, crushed
> Olive oil for brushing
> 16 large grape leaves (see Note)
> Lemon wedges for serving

Prepare a hot fire in a grill. Lightly season the chops with salt and pepper and rub each side of the chops with the garlic. Brush with a little olive oil. Brown the meat over a very hot fire—do not cook through! Simply "grill mark" the chops on both sides and remove to cool. The lamb should still be raw in the center.

Rinse the grape leaves in cold water and drain. Pat them dry with paper towels, being careful not to tear the leaves. Trim off any thick stems and discard. Arrange the leaves in overlapping pairs on the countertop. Place a cooled chop on each pair of leaves and wrap the leaves around the meat, leaving the bone exposed. Secure with toothpicks. Brush on both sides with olive oil. Grill over high heat for 1 to 2 minutes on each side for medium-rare. Remove the toothpicks, and serve with lemon wedges.

NOTE: Purchase grape leaves packed in water in glass jars in Middle Eastern or specialty shops.

This recipe can also be done on a stove-top grill, but the charcoal barbecue adds that special taste.

Grilled Lamb Chops with Mint and Cinnamon in Grape Leaves

Serves 4

The addition of mint and cinnamon to this dish gives it that sweet Middle Eastern flavor. When I described this dish to Craig, our chef, he prepared it and called me to the kitchen. We tasted the chops and then Craig immediately said, "Please, Smith, don't make me change a thing!" They are that good.

> **8 lamb rib chops (about 3 to 4 ounces each), trimmed of excess fat**
>
> **Salt and freshly ground black pepper to taste**
>
> **Olive oil for brushing**
>
> **1/2 teaspoon dried mint**
>
> **Pinch of ground cinnamon**
>
> **16 large grape leaves (see Note)**

Prepare a hot fire in a grill. Lightly season the chops with salt and pepper and brush on both sides with a little olive oil. Brown the chops quickly on both sides in a very hot fire—do not cook through! Simply "grill mark" the chops on both sides and remove to cool. The lamb chops should still be raw in the center.

Sprinkle both sides of the chops with the dried mint and cinnamon. (Easy on the cinnamon!)

Rinse the grape leaves in cold water and drain. Pat them dry with paper towels, being careful not to tear the leaves. Trim off any thick stems and discard. Arrange the leaves in overlapping pairs on the countertop. Place a chop on each pair of leaves and wrap the leaves around the meat, leaving the bone exposed. Secure the leaves with toothpicks. Brush on both sides with olive oil. Grill the chops over high heat for 1 to 2 minutes on each side for medium-rare. Remove the toothpicks before serving.

NOTE: Purchase grape leaves packed in water in glass jars in Middle Eastern or specialty shops.

This can also be done on a stove-top grill, but the charcoal barbecue adds that special taste.

Boiled Beef

Since meat was either boiled or roasted in ancient Israel we should consider the old boiled brisket bit. The Pascal Lamb was always roasted, as it still is in Israel and all portions of the Eastern Orthodox Church. In Rome, however, the roasting of meat was considered sort of a peasant thing, and thus boiled meat was preferred.

It is easier and much more economical to boil rather than roast red meat, since much less fuel and attention are necessary. I love boiled beef and lamb. I even do turkey this way.

Simply place the brisket, pot roast, or beef shank into a pot with a tight-fitting lid. Add some parsley sprigs, chopped garlic, bay leaves, and thyme. Cover the meat with water, cover the pot, and bring to a simmer. Cook gently until done to taste.

This is simple, ancient, tasty, convenient, and healthful, since you are getting rid of fat—and you come up with a great soup stock besides. Remember, nothing in the ancient world was wasted. Impossible!

Braised Beef with Apricots and Figs

Serves 6 to 8

In this recipe, I brown the meat first and then braise it in a pot. This dish is sweet and rich because of the dried fruit, so it serves more than you might expect. This is a great way to get your family, especially the kids, to eat less meat and enjoy it more. You'll want to set up a tent in the backyard and eat with your fingers while sitting on a Persian rug. So rich!

1 4-pound beef brisket

Salt and freshly ground black pepper to taste

2 tablespoons olive oil

2 medium yellow onions, peeled and coarsely chopped

$^1/_4$ cup chopped fresh parsley

2 cups Beef Stock (page 120)

1 cup water

Juice of 1 lemon

$1^1/_2$ cinnamon sticks

2 tablespoons distilled white vinegar

1 tablespoon honey

2 cups dried figs

$1^1/_2$ cups dried apricots

Season the brisket lightly with salt and pepper and rub with the olive oil. Place the meat fatty side up on a rack in a large roasting pan. Brown the beef in a preheated 475° oven for 25 minutes. Remove the meat on the rack and set aside.

Add the onions to the roasting pan and set the meat (without the rack) on top. Add the parsley, stock, water, lemon juice, and cinnamon sticks. Cover the pan with a lid or aluminum foil and return to the oven. Reduce the temperature to 300° and bake for 2 hours and 15 minutes. Remove the pan from the oven.

Mix the vinegar and honey together and pour over the meat. Add the dried figs and apricots. Cover and bake for 1 hour and 15 minutes more, until very tender. Turn the meat in the fruit sauce a couple of times while baking.

Add salt and pepper to taste to the sauce. Slice the meat across the grain and serve with the sauce.

Braised Beef with Apricots and Mulberries

Serves 6 to 8

Another heart- and tummy-warming dish filled with the sweetness of dried fruit. Dried mulberries are available in Middle Eastern markets. If you cannot find them, you can substitute a mixture of fresh blackberries and raspberries. Mulberries have a similar flavor to such a blend, though mulberries are a tad more sour. I really enjoy them. You might even find them fresh in the late summer, early fall berry season. Look in farmers' markets.

1 4-pound beef brisket

Salt and freshly ground black pepper to taste

3 medium yellow onions, peeled and coarsely chopped

2 tablespoons chopped fresh parsley

2 cups Beef Stock (page 120)

1 cup water

Juice of 1 lemon

1½ cinnamon sticks

½ cup dried apricots

1 cup dried mulberries (page 99)

2 tablespoons distilled white vinegar

Season the brisket lightly with salt and pepper. Place the meat fatty side up on a rack in a large roasting pan. Brown the beef in a preheated 475° oven for 25 minutes. Remove the meat on the rack and set aside.

Add the onions to the roasting pan and set the meat (without the rack) on top. Add the parsley, stock, water, lemon juice, and cinnamon sticks. Cover the pan with a lid or aluminum foil and return to the oven. Reduce the temperature to 300° and bake for 2 hours and 15 minutes.

Add the apricots, cover, and bake for 30 minutes more. Add the mullberries and vinegar, cover, and bake for 30 minutes more, turning the meat in the fruit sauce a couple of times. Add salt and pepper to taste to the sauce. Slice the meat across the grain and serve with the sauce.

Braised Beef with Apricots and Raspberries

Serves 6 to 8

If you are Jewish you will probably claim that this tastes a lot like your Grandma's tzimmes. If you are not Jewish, then you are in for a sweet treat. This method of cooking beef goes back a thousand years in terms of Jewish traditions and in this recipe we have used items that are all readily available. Try it and enjoy!

> 1 4-pound beef brisket
>
> Salt and freshly ground black pepper to taste
>
> 2 medium yellow onions, peeled and coarsely chopped
>
> 1/4 cup chopped fresh parsley
>
> 2 cups Beef Stock (page 120)
>
> 1 cup water
>
> Juice of 1 lemon
>
> 1 cinnamon stick, broken in half
>
> 3/4 cup dried apricots
>
> 1 1/2 cups red raspberries, fresh or frozen
>
> 2 tablespoons distilled white vinegar

Season the brisket lightly with salt and pepper. Place the meat fatty side up on a rack in a large roasting pan. Brown the beef in a preheated 475° oven for 25 minutes. Remove the meat on the rack and set aside.

Add the onions to the roasting pan and top with the browned meat (without the rack). Add the parsley, stock, water, lemon juice, and cinnamon stick. Cover the pan with a lid or aluminum foil and return to the oven. Reduce the temperature to 300° and bake for 2 hours and 15 minutes.

Add the apricots, cover, and bake for another 45 minutes.

Add the raspberries and vinegar, cover, and bake for 15 minutes more, or until the raspberries have cooked down into the sauce. Turn the meat in the fruit sauce a couple of times.

Add salt and pepper to taste to the sauce. Slice the meat across the grain and serve with the sauce from the pan.

Braised Beef with Mulberries and Pomegranate Molasses

Serves 6 to 8

Two sours don't make a sweet!" I am not so sure. In this dish we used two rather tart fruit products and the results are surprisingly sweet but not at all heavy. This is one of my favorite beef dishes.

1 4-pound beef brisket

Salt and freshly ground black pepper to taste

2 tablespoons olive oil

3 cloves garlic, chopped

2 medium yellow onions, peeled and chopped

1½ cups Beef Stock (page 120)

½ cup dry white wine

1 cup dried mulberries (page 99)

2 tablespoons pomegranate molasses (available in Middle Eastern markets)

Season the beef with salt and pepper to taste. Heat a large frying pan and add 1 tablespoon of the oil. Brown the beef on both sides, and place in a large stove-top casserole.

Heat the frying pan again and add the remaining 1 tablespoon oil, the garlic, and onions. Sauté for 5 minutes and add to the beef. Add the beef stock and wine. Bring to a boil, cover, and simmer gently for 3 hours, turning the meat a few times while cooking.

Add the remaining ingredients and simmer, covered, for 20 minutes more. Adjust the salt if needed. Slice the meat across the grain and serve with the sauce spooned over it.

Beef Pot Roast with Onions, Leeks, and Pomegranate Molasses

Serves 4 to 6

Pot roast is one of those dear comfort foods from our childhood that brings back wonderful memories every time we prepare it. This version uses the usual ingredients along with a shot of pomegranate molasses. The concentrated fruit syrup brings a refreshing sort of sourness to the dish, an appreciated change.

1 3½-pound beef pot roast

Salt and freshly ground black pepper to taste

2 tablespoons olive oil

2 cloves garlic, chopped

1 medium yellow onion, peeled and coarsely chopped

4 cups cleaned and coarsely chopped leeks
  (white part only)

1 cup Beef Stock (page 120)

½ cup dry white wine

⅓ cup pomegranate molasses (available in Middle Eastern
  markets)

Season the meat with salt and pepper to taste. Heat a large nonstick frying pan and add 1 tablespoon of the oil. Brown the beef on all sides, and remove to a 6-quart stove-top casserole.

Heat the pan again and add the remaining 1 tablespoon oil, the garlic, and onions. Sauté for 2 minutes. Add the leeks and sauté for 2 minutes more. Add to the casserole along with the beef stock and wine. Bring to a boil, cover, and simmer gently for 1 hour and 15 minutes.

Add the pomegranate molasses and simmer for 30 minutes more. Add salt and pepper to taste. Slice the meat across the grain and serve with the sauce.

Beef Stew with Almond Curd Sauce

Serves 6

This dish is from an interesting volume called *The Good Book Cookbook*. The spices and pomegranate molasses take you back to the desert.

> 3 pounds boneless beef stewing meat, cut into 1-inch pieces
>
> Salt and freshly ground black pepper to taste
>
> 3 tablespoons olive oil
>
> 1¹⁄₂ cups Chicken Stock (page 118)
>
> ¹⁄₂ cup dry white wine
>
> ¹⁄₂ cinnamon stick
>
> ¹⁄₂ cup blanched whole almonds
>
> 2 cloves garlic, peeled
>
> 1¹⁄₂ teaspoons ground cumin
>
> 1¹⁄₂ teaspoons ground coriander
>
> ¹⁄₄ teaspoon salt
>
> ¹⁄₄ cup water
>
> 1 large yellow onion, peeled and thinly sliced
>
> 1 cup plain yogurt, Homemade (page 204) or from the market
>
> 2 teaspoons pomegranate molasses (available in Middle Eastern markets)

Season the beef with salt and pepper to taste. Brown the meat in two batches in a large frying pan using 1 tablespoon of the oil each time. Remove the meat to a 4- to 6-quart pot. Deglaze the pan with $1/2$ cup of the stock. Add to the beef along with the wine, cinnamon stick, and the remaining 1 cup stock set aside. Wipe out the pan with a paper towel.

Heat the frying pan again and toast the almonds over low heat until golden brown. Allow to cool and coarsely chop. Place the almonds in a food blender along with the garlic, cumin, coriander, and salt. Blend for a few seconds to mix, and add the water. Blend to form a paste. Add a little more water to facilitate blending if necessary. Set aside.

Heat the frying pan again and add the remaining 1 table-spoon olive oil. Add the onion and sauté for 3 minutes. Add the almond paste, stir, and cook for 2 minutes. Add to the pot of meat, stir together and bring to a simmer. Cover and simmer for about $2^{1}/_{2}$ hours, until the meat is tender. Remove from the heat.

Mix the yogurt and pomegranate molasses together and stir into the stew. Add salt and pepper to taste. Return the pot to the burner and heat gently; do not boil.

Birds and Game

The chicken, that most beloved of all American table birds, was probably not known in ancient Palestine. What we know as our domestic chicken is probably descended from a wild bird in Southeast Asia. A domesticated bird was common among the Chinese as early as 200 B.C. It spread through Greece to Rome, so the Romans knew of such a bird, but it did not appear until later in Palestine.

In the early days we do see mention of game birds in the Old Testament. They refer to quail, squab (or pigeons), turtledoves, and some sort of a wild bird that ran about in the region.

We have used birds that can be found in your local market in the following recipes. Oh, your butcher is out of turtledoves? Try Rock Cornish game hen, a hybrid of the Cornish hen and White Rock hens. They are moist, easy to cook, and often can be found on sale in the supermarkets. All of the recipes for small birds in this section can be adapted for Cornish game hens.

However, if you have never prepared squab or quail, you are in for a treat. These can be found in fancy butcher shops, where they tend to be a bit expensive. But try shopping in Chinatown—you will find them at much better prices, as the Chinese love these small birds.

We offer chicken in place of whatever that "fowl" was that is mentioned in the Bible. Eggs were eaten in Biblical times, which makes me wonder how often the fowl were killed for food—since you would have to give up your egg source. We never think of these problems in our time since we raise all kinds of birds for cooking and others just for the laying of eggs.

These recipes are not at all complex. As soon as you find a source for squab and quail, you will be all set. Do not miss Fowl with Grapes or Quail Simmered in Fruit Sauce.

Fowl with Grapes

Serves 4 to 5

In the old days, I suppose, you would serve this some evening when a wealthy friend from Persia appeared on your doorstep. This is very rich and certainly worth your effort. Black caraway seed is not what we call caraway seed. You can find black caraway seed, a necessary element in this dish, in Middle Eastern grocery stores.

2 1³/₄-pound Cornish game hens (thawed if frozen), cut into quarters

Salt and freshly ground black pepper to taste

2 tablespoons olive oil

1 cup thinly sliced yellow onion

1 teaspoon anise seed

1 teaspoon black caraway seed (find in Middle Eastern markets)

¹/₂ cup dry white wine

¹/₂ cup Chicken Stock (page 118)

2 teaspoons honey

1 cup seedless green grapes

Season the game hens with salt and pepper to taste. Heat a large frying pan and add 1 tablespoon of the oil. Brown the game hens on both sides and place in a 4- to 6-quart pot. Discard the fat.

Heat the frying pan again and add the remaining 1 table-spoon oil. Add the onion and sauté for 5 minutes. Add to the game hens. Set aside.

Heat a small frying pan and toast the anise and black car-away seed over low heat for a few minutes. Do not burn. Place the toasted seeds in a mortar with a pestle and crush coarsely. Add to the game hens along with the white wine and chicken stock. Bring to a simmer, cover, and simmer gently for 20 min-utes, turning the game hens a couple of times.

Add the honey and grapes, cover, and simmer for 15 minutes more. Remove the game hens to a warm serving platter.

Bring the pot of sauce with the grapes to a boil and simmer for a few minutes to thicken slightly. Add salt and pepper to taste, and pour the sauce and grapes over the hens.

Fowl Stuffed with Bulgur Wheat Dressing

Serves 2 to 4

This sort of poultry stuffing has been around a long time. A Jewish friend of mine does a similar thing with kasha (buckwheat groats). The Lebanese and Syrians stuff birds with rice and spices.

We are fond of the basic flavors in this dish. If you wish to substitute pine nuts for the almonds, go right ahead. That may be even better.

1 cup Chicken Stock (page 118)

$^1/_2$ cup coarse-ground bulgur wheat

$^1/_2$ teaspoon salt, plus more to taste

$^1/_4$ cup slivered almonds, toasted

$1^1/_2$ tablespoons olive oil

1 cup finely chopped yellow onion

1 tablespoon chopped fresh parsley

$^1/_4$ teaspoon ground cinnamon

Freshly ground black pepper to taste

2 $1^3/_4$-pound game hens (thawed, if frozen)

Combine the chicken stock, bulgur wheat, and salt in a small saucepan and bring to a boil. Cover and simmer gently for 10 minutes. Remove the pan from the stove and allow to cool, uncovered, so that the bulgur absorbs all the liquid.

Heat a small frying pan and toast the almonds over low heat until golden brown. Remove the almonds to a plate to cool.

Heat the frying pan again and add the oil and onion. Sauté until just tender. Place the cooled bulgur in a bowl and add the toasted almonds and the onion. Add the remaining ingredients except the hens and mix together well.

Stuff the birds with the mixture and tie the legs together with kitchen string. Tuck the wings underneath the hens and season the hens with salt and pepper to taste. Place on a rack in a roasting pan and roast in a preheated 375° oven for 1 hour and 15 minutes. Allow the hens to rest for 5 minutes before serving.

Fowl Stuffed with Barley and Mustard Green Dressing

Serves 4 to 6

The use of mustard greens must have been common in ancient times, and certainly there was plenty of barley. So Craig and I came up with this one, and we were very pleasantly surprised. This is easy, filling, and rich, all at once.

    1/2 cup barley, rinsed and drained
    1 tablespoon butter
    2 cloves garlic
    1 cup finely chopped yellow onion
    4 cups coarsely chopped mustard greens (washed)
    1 egg, lightly beaten
    Salt and freshly ground black pepper to taste
    4 1 1/2-pound Cornish game hens (thawed, if frozen)
    1 teaspoon ground cumin

Place the barley in a steamer basket lined with cheesecloth and steam for 2 hours. Add water to the bottom of the steamer as necessary. Remove to a large bowl and allow to cool.

Heat a frying pan and add the butter, garlic, and onion. Sauté until the onion is tender. Add the mustard greens and sauté for 3 minutes more. Combine the cooled barley and the sautéed vegetables in a bowl. Add the beaten egg and salt and pepper to taste, and mix well.

Stuff the birds with the barley mixture. Tie the legs together with kitchen string. Tuck the wings underneath the hens and season with the ground cumin and salt and pepper to taste. Place on a rack in a roasting pan and roast in a preheated 375° oven for 1 to 1 1/4 hours. Allow the hens to rest for 5 minutes before serving.

Quail with Garlic and Cumin

Serves 4

This is one of the quickest ways that I know of obtaining a really flavorful quail in the least amount of time. This recipe was specifically designed for quail, but squab can be done in the same way.

If you are using squab, use one per person and cook them a bit longer on each side as they are larger than the little quail.

Use a stove-top grill for this, one of those ribbed black metal grills, or use a plain old black frying pan.

8 quail (about 4 to 6 ounces each)

4 cloves garlic, crushed

1 tablespoon ground cumin

2 tablespoons olive oil

Salt and freshly ground black pepper to taste

Butterfly the quail by cutting them down the back with kitchen scissors (do not cut down the breasts, or the birds will dry out while cooking). Flatten the cut quail and place on a baking sheet. Rub both sides of the quail with the remaining ingredients, and allow to marinate for 30 minutes. Grill over high heat for about 2 to 3 minutes per side.

Squab or Game Hens with Spices

Serves 4 to 6

This recipe looks much more complicated than it actually is. Just relax and read through it and then be prepared to give your family and guests a meal over which they will marvel. This is a grand blend of some of the spices available in the ancient world, available if you were rich, and in terms of food sources and costs, in our time we are very rich!

GAME HENS

2 1½-pound Cornish game hens (thawed, if frozen)

¼ cup chopped fresh parsley

3 cloves garlic, chopped

1 teaspoon salt

½ teaspoon saffron

1½ teaspoons freshly ground coriander seed

¼ teaspoon ground cumin

1 medium yellow onion, peeled and finely chopped

1 teaspoon grated ginger root

2 cinnamon sticks, broken in half

1 piece lemon peel (2 inches long by ½ inch wide with no pith)

1 cup water

¼ cup dry white wine

2 tablespoons butter

¼ cup pine nuts, toasted (see Note)

BULGUR WHEAT

1 tablespoon olive oil

1 cup coarse-ground bulgur wheat (page 98)

1 teaspoon salt

2 cups Chicken Stock (page 118)

EGG MIXTURE

3 eggs

1 tablespoon butter

2 teaspoons fresh lemon juice

Salt and freshly ground black pepper to taste

Place the game hens in a 4- to 6-quart pot and add the remaining ingredients for the hens except the pine nuts. Bring to a boil, cover, and simmer for 45 minutes. Remove the birds from the pot and allow to cool. Remove the cinnamon sticks and discard.

Remove the meat from the bones and pull into large strips. Discard the bones. Return the meat to the pot of sauce and add the toasted pine nuts. Set aside.

Heat a small saucepan and add the oil and bulgur. Lightly brown the bulgur. Add the salt and chicken stock. Bring to a boil, cover, and simmer for 20 minutes, until tender.

In a medium frying pan, scramble the eggs in the butter. Do not overcook, as the eggs should be moist. When done, add the lemon juice and salt and pepper to taste.

Reheat the pot of sauce and meat until hot. Don't boil this too heavily or the meat will toughen. Gently stir in the scrambled eggs. Serve over the bulgur wheat.

NOTE: Simply toast the pine nuts in a frying pan with a tiny bit of oil until they are golden brown, not dark.

Quail Simmered in Fruit Sauce

Serves 4

This is a most elegant dish yet not at all difficult to prepare. I taste the desert winds on a fall evening when I eat this. I only serve it to people who I really appreciate, or to really serious eaters.

You can find apricot nectar in the fruit juice section of your supermarket. It may come in those new fancy little lunch sack jar types.

Please do not overcook these little birds.

8 quail (about 6 ounces each)

Salt and freshly ground black pepper to taste

2 tablespoons olive oil

2 cups apricot nectar

$1/2$ cup dry white wine

$1/4$ cup golden raisins

2 teaspoons pomegranate molasses (available in Middle Eastern markets)

Butterfly the quail by cutting them down the back with kitchen scissors. Open up the birds and flatten them on the countertop, skin side up. Season the birds on both sides with salt and pepper to taste. Heat a large frying pan and add the oil. Add the quail, skin side down (you may have to do this in a couple of batches). Brown the birds over medium-high heat for about 1 to 2 minutes on each side. Remove to a baking sheet to cool.

Heat the pan again and add the remaining ingredients. Bring to a boil. Add the browned quail and simmer gently, covered, for about 25 minutes, or until the quail are just cooked through and tender. Turn the birds a couple of times as the sauce in the pan begins to reduce and thicken. Add salt and pepper to taste. Remove from the heat and allow to rest, covered, for 5 minutes before serving.

Chicken with Quince Jam and Wine

Serves 4

For this one you will have to find quince jam, if you don't make it yourself. It is available in some Middle Eastern markets. It gives the chicken a most delightful and almost mysterious flavor since it is hard to put your finger on all of the flavors that a quince offers.

> 1 3½-pound chicken, rinsed, dried, and cut into 8 serving pieces
>
> Kosher salt and freshly ground black pepper to taste
>
> 2 tablespoons olive oil
>
> 1 medium yellow onion, peeled and thinly sliced
>
> ½ cup Chicken Stock (page 118)
>
> ½ cup dry white wine
>
> 1½ tablespoons fresh lemon juice
>
> ¾ cup Quince Jam (page 284) (or find in Middle Eastern markets)
>
> 1 tablespoon chopped fresh parsley

Season the chicken with salt and pepper to taste. Heat a large frying pan and add 1 tablespoon of the oil. Add the chicken and brown on both sides. Remove to a 6-quart stove-top casserole.

Heat the frying pan again and add the remaining 1 tablespoon oil. Add the onions and sauté for 5 minutes. Add to the chicken. Add the remaining ingredients and bring to a boil. Cover and simmer gently for 40 minutes, or until cooked through. Turn the pieces of chicken a couple of times while cooking. Add salt and pepper to taste.

Chicken with Olives and Leeks

Serves 4

This is a very old dish that is still served in parts of Italy and Greece, as well as the Middle East. There is no way that we can emphasize the importance of the olive tree in the ancient world. Food, oil, flavor, it was all there!

1 3½-pound chicken, rinsed, dried, and cut into 8 serving pieces

Salt and freshly ground black pepper to taste

1 cup all-purpose flour

4 cups julienned leeks (white part only)

3 tablespoons olive oil

4 cloves garlic, crushed

1 6-ounce jar pitted small green olives (without pimentos), drained

¼ cup chopped fresh parsley

1 cup Chicken Stock (page 118)

½ cup dry white wine

Season the chicken with salt and pepper to taste. Place the chicken in a bowl and add the flour. Coat the chicken pieces with the flour and pat off the excess. Set the chicken aside.

Cut off the ends of the leeks and discard. Julienne the white part only of the leeks into 3-inch-long pieces. Discard the green tops. Wash very carefully and set aside.

Heat a large frying pan and brown the chicken in 2 batches using 1 tablespoon of the oil each time. Remove to a 4- to 6-quart stove-top casserole.

Heat the frying pan again and add the remaining 1 tablespoon oil, the garlic, and leeks. Sauté for 3 minutes and add to the chicken. Add remaining ingredients. Bring to a boil, cover, and simmer gently for about 30 minutes, until the chicken is cooked through. Add salt and pepper to taste.

Roasted Chicken with Quince Glaze

Serves 4

This dish is deceptively simple. You cannot imagine how delicious the roasted skin of a chicken covered with quince jam is. You have to try this!

1 3¹/₂-pound chicken, rinsed and dried

Kosher salt and freshly ground black pepper to taste

¹/₂ cup Quince Jam (page 284; or find in Middle Eastern markets)

¹/₂ cup water

Season the bird with salt and pepper to taste. Tie the legs together with kitchen string and tuck the wings underneath the chicken. Place on a rack in a roasting pan. Roast in a preheated 375° oven for 45 minutes.

Meanwhile, combine the quince jam and water in a saucepan and simmer until syrupy, about 10 minutes. Set aside.

After the initial 45 minutes of roasting, reduce the oven temperature to 350° and brush the chicken with some of the quince syrup. Continue roasting for 30 minutes more, brushing the bird every 10 minutes with the remaining syrup. Allow the chicken to rest in a warm place for 5 minutes before carving and serving.

Fish in
Biblical Times

Since I am a child of Seattle, it is very hard for me to imagine a people who had little fish to eat. Such was the case in Old Testament times. Consider the fact that the Children of Israel rarely controlled the Mediterranean coast and they therefore had to depend upon the Sea of Galilee for fish, not a rich source then or now. Further, transportation was so slow that it was impossible to get fresh fish into the major cities or villages. One had to go to the sea! So while in the wilderness, the Hebrews longed for the fish they had known during captivity in Egypt.

In New Testament times, fish seems to have been more common, or at least it is mentioned more often. The miracle of the loaves and fishes, with the appearance of Jesus beside the Sea of Galilee, eating a fish luncheon with his followers, attests to the presence of fish among the peoples of that time. Indeed, several of Jesus' disciples were fishermen.

The following fish recipes are rather plain, since I think that is the way that fish was cooked in those days. Oh, we have a fancy one in Fish with Vinegar, Oil, and Saffron, but the others are pretty straightforward, yet delicious nevertheless.

Fish with Vinegar, Oil, and Saffron

Serves 4 to 6

This is somewhat unusual. What you have here is a fried fish pickled in vinegar and saffron. It comes from the Abruzzi, the only region in Italy where saffron grows, yet it tastes like a dish that must have been the rage among the wealthy classes in ancient Palestine. They were the only ones who could afford fresh fish and saffron, and so I suppose that this sort of thing would have fit right in!

1 cup white wine vinegar

2 cloves garlic, sliced

1 cup thinly sliced yellow onion

Pinch of saffron

$1/2$ cup water

2 tablespoons fresh lemon juice

$1^{1}/2$ pounds skinless fresh cod fillets

Salt and freshly ground black pepper to taste

1 cup unbleached all-purpose flour

2 to 3 cups olive oil, for frying

GARNISHES

Lettuce leaves

Sliced red onions

Capers

Combine the ingredients for the marinade in a small saucepan and bring to a boil. Simmer, uncovered, for 2 minutes. Remove to a medium bowl to cool.

Cut the fish crosswise into $1^{1}/2$-inch pieces. Season lightly with salt and pepper to taste. Dredge the fish in the flour and pat off the excess.

In a large frying pan, heat about 1 inch of olive oil to 375° (an electric frying pan is great for this). Fry the fish until golden brown on all sides. Remove to paper towels to drain.

Add the fried fish to the marinade and carefully toss together. Cover and refrigerate for several hours, or overnight.

Drain and discard the marinade. Serve the fish garnished with the lettuce leaves, sliced red onions, and capers.

Broiled Fish
with Honey and Oil

Serves 4

Most of us would not ever think of cooking fish with honey and oil, but this was common in the ancient Middle East. It is also common in our time in China. They seem to have always done it first.

4 6- to 8-ounce halibut steaks, about 1 inch thick
Salt and freshly ground black pepper to taste
2 tablespoons honey
2 tablespoons olive oil

Preheat the broiler. Season the fish with salt and pepper to taste. Rub the fish on both sides with the honey, then rub with the oil. Place the fish on a nonstick baking sheet. Place the oven rack in the upper shelf. Broil the fish for 4 to 5 minutes per side, until just firm.

Broiled Fish
with Garlic and Mint

Serves 4

Simplicity is sometimes the very best thing in the kitchen. This is as simple as you can get, and the results will always be appreciated.

4 6- to 8-ounce halibut steaks, about 1 inch thick

Salt and freshly ground black pepper to taste

2 cloves garlic, crushed

1 tablespoon chopped fresh mint

Season the halibut with salt and pepper to taste. Rub the fish on both sides with the garlic and mint and allow to marinate for 30 minutes.

Preheat the broiler. Place the steaks on an oiled nonstick baking sheet. Place the pan on the upper shelf of an oven with an active broiler. Broil the fish for 4 to 5 minutes on each side, until just firm. Do not overcook.

Fish Wrapped in Vine Leaves

Serves 4

I do not like fish that is overcooked; it should be moist and a bit firm, never mushy. This recipe will help you achieve such results. I have not tried this yet with salmon, our Northwest treasure, but I am willing to believe that this method will work with any kind of fish.

Since we know that during times of famine grape leaves were commonly eaten in the ancient world, we can assume that this method of cooking was not uncommon.

4 6- to 8-ounce halibut steaks, about 1 inch thick

Salt and freshly ground black pepper to taste

3 tablespoons olive oil

2 tablespoons fresh lemon juice

2 tablespoons chopped fresh dill

16 large grape leaves (see Note)

Olive oil for grilling

Season the fish with salt and pepper to taste. Place the fish in a shallow dish along with the olive oil, lemon juice, and dill. Turn the fish to coat and allow to marinate for 30 minutes.

Prepare a hot fire in a charcoal grill. Rinse the grape leaves in cold water and pat dry on paper towels. Trim off the tough stems from the leaves if they exist. Lay the leaves out on a countertop in overlapping groups of 4 to form a square. Place a fish steak in the center of each group of leaves and wrap the leaves around the fish, like an envelope, making as tight a package as possible. Secure the leaves with toothpicks. Brush the leaves with olive oil. Grill the fish over a very hot charcoal grill for about 3 minutes on each side. The fish should be firm but not overcooked. Sprinkle with salt to taste and serve.

NOTE: Purchase grape leaves packed in water in glass jars in Middle Eastern markets or specialty shops.

Vegetables in
Biblical Times

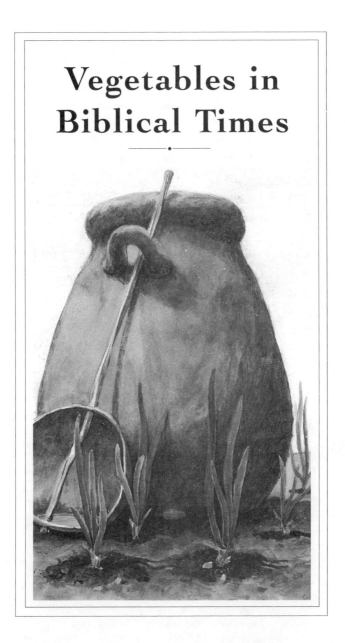

P oor Moses. He really did not know where he was going. People of great faith rarely know where they are going to end up, but the Children of Israel wanted to know where they were going. Isn't it interesting that Moses basically said, "Come on, this way!" and we followed, not knowing where we were going.

But there came a time during the flight from Egypt to the Promised Land when the Children of Israel became downright snippy with Moses, and their complaint tells us something about the vegetables that they knew at the time.

Now the rabble that was among them had a strong craving; and the people of Israel also wept again, and said, "O that we had meat to eat! We remember the fish we ate in Egypt for nothing, the cucumbers, the melons, the leeks, the onions, and the garlic; but now our strength is dried up, and there is nothing at all but this manna to look at." (Numbers 11:4–5)

Palestine was not a great place for farming, so we know how scarce vegetables were even during good times. The cucumbers, garlic, onions, and leeks the people could grow, as these are rather tough plants, but more delicate plants such as lettuce and tender greens were impossible to raise in the desert.

We have tried to use only those vegetables that were common to the people of Israel during those ancient times, times of waiting and hoping and hunger.

(See the list of Biblical Foods on page 95 for more information.)

Sautéed Onions and Leeks

Serves 4 to 6 as a side vegetable dish

This may sound a little exotic for ancient times, but please remember that if you could afford the goods, the possibilities were quite bright. The only problem is that very few people could afford such things. We are lucky that we Americans can now afford to taste almost anything in the world.

4 cups julienned leeks (white part only)

1/4 cup slivered almonds, toasted

2 tablespoons olive oil

2 medium yellow onions, peeled and thinly sliced

1 tablespoon chopped fresh parsley

1 tablespoon chopped fresh sage

1/4 cup dry white wine

Salt and freshly ground black pepper to taste

Cut off the green tops of the leeks and discard. Julienne only the white part of the leeks, cutting 3-inch by 1/8-inch strips. Rinse the leeks and drain well. Place the almonds in a small frying pan and toast over low heat until golden brown; shake the frying pan so that the almonds do not burn. Set aside.

Heat a large frying pan and add the oil and onions. Sauté until the onions are almost transparent. Add the leeks, parsley, sage, and toasted almonds. Sauté for 2 minutes. Add the wine and salt and pepper to taste. Cook for 1 to 2 minutes more, until all is tender.

Stuffed Onion Leaves, Old World Style

Serves 6 to 8 as a side dish

This dish will become very popular with your family, I warn you. Variations on this dish are found in several Middle Eastern cultures, and we can assume that it is very old. This one takes a bit of time, but it will prove to be a smash hit at your Biblical dinner party.

1/2 cup fine-ground bulgur wheat

4 large yellow onions (about 4 pounds)

1 pound ground lamb

1/3 cup yogurt, Homemade (page 204) or from the market

1 tablespoon chopped fresh dill

1 teaspoon ground cumin

1/4 teaspoon ground cinnamon

Salt and freshly ground black pepper to taste

1 tablespoon olive oil

1/3 cup Chicken Stock (page 118)

Place the bulgur in a small bowl and add 1 cup cold water. Allow to sit for 45 minutes.

Place the whole unpeeled onions in a large pot and just barely cover with water. Bring to a boil, reduce the heat, and simmer, covered, for 20 minutes. Drain the onions and allow to cool.

Cut the tops and bottoms off the cooked onions. Slice into each onion by making a cut down the side of the onion through to the center. Remove and discard the outer skin. Then very carefully remove the outer layers, or "leaves," of the onion (save the centers of the onions, cores, for some other dish). You should get 5 or 6 leaves from each large onion.

Drain the bulgur well, and place in a bowl. Add the ground lamb, yogurt, dill, spices, and salt and pepper to taste, and mix well. Place about 3 tablespoons of the lamb mixture in each onion leaf and roll it up to form a fat sausage (the leaves will practically roll themselves together).

Heat a large frying pan and add the olive oil. Place the onion rolls seam side down in the pan and cook over medium heat for about 5 minutes. Add the stock, cover, and simmer gently for about 40 minutes, or until all the liquid is absorbed.

Leek Fritters with Garlic

Makes 6 fritters

No wonder the Children of Israel were so upset that they had no leeks or garlic during the flight from Egypt to the New Land. These two flavors just seem to belong together, and the resulting fritter goes with just everything.

4 cups cleaned thinly sliced leeks (white part only)

1 tablespoon olive oil

3 cloves garlic, crushed

1 tablespoon chopped fresh parsley

3 eggs, beaten

1 tablespoon all-purpose flour

Salt and freshly ground black pepper to taste

Olive oil for panfrying

Cut off the bottoms of the leeks and discard. Thinly slice the white part only of the leeks. Rinse and drain well. Discard the dark green tops of the leeks.

Heat a large frying pan and add the oil, garlic, and leeks. Sauté quickly over high heat for 3 minutes. Remove to a bowl to cool.

Add the remaining ingredients to the bowl and mix together.

Heat a large nonstick frying pan and add the oil for frying. Measure out 1/2-cup quantities of the fritter mixture and add to the hot pan. Flatten each one slightly and fry over medium heat until golden brown on both sides. (You will have to do this in batches so there is ample room in the frying pan.) Add more oil, if necessary. Remove to drain on paper towels, and serve hot.

Fried Cucumbers with Sesame Oil and Coriander

Serves 4 as a side dish

We do not think of flavor blends like this in our time. I put this together because the ingredients would have been available in ancient times, and I was amazed at the outcome. We have so much to learn from the ancient cooks!

2 medium cucumbers (about 1½ pounds)

2 tablespoons butter

Salt and freshly ground black pepper to taste

2 teaspoons toasted sesame oil

1 tablespoon chopped fresh coriander

Trim off the ends of the cucumbers and slice the cucumbers crosswise ⅛ inch thick (a mandoline works great for this). Line a baking sheet with a few layers of paper towels and place a single layer of cucumber slices on to absorb some of their water. Add another layer of paper towels and another layer of cucumbers and continue with the remaining cucumbers, ending with a layer of paper towels. Allow to drain for 1 hour, then discard the paper towels.

Heat a large frying pan and melt the butter. Panfry the cucumbers and salt and pepper to taste, tossing over medium-high heat for 5 minutes, or until lightly browned. Add the sesame oil and coriander and toss again.

Fried Cucumbers
with Hyssop

Serves 4 as a side dish

Talk about simple, and yet very old. Please tell your children about the history of these foods when you serve them. The tongue remembers better than the brain!

2 medium cucumbers (about 1½ pounds)

3 tablespoons butter

2 tablespoons chopped fresh hyssop (see Note)

Salt and freshly ground black pepper to taste

Trim off the ends of the cucumbers and discard. Slice the cucumbers crosswise ⅛ inch thick (a mandoline works great for this). Line a baking sheet with a few layers of paper towels and place a single layer of cucumber slices on top. Add another layer of paper towels and another layer of cucumbers. Lay another layer of paper towels on top and lightly press on the cucumbers. Allow to drain for at least 30 minutes. Remove the cucumbers to a bowl and discard the paper towels.

Heat a large frying pan and melt the butter. Add the drained cucumbers and fry over medium-high heat with the remaining ingredients for about 5 minutes. Toss together while cooking to brown slightly.

NOTE: If you don't grow your own hyssop, substitute 1 tablespoon each fresh mint and fresh thyme. Or use 1 tablespoon dried hyssop (page 99) from a good herb and spice shop.

Fried Cucumbers
with Sumac

Serves 4 as a side vegetable dish

When Craig and I thought about whether or not someone in ancient times would have enjoyed a dish such as this, we simply decided that we enjoyed it and thus it qualified for this collection. It is very good; but then sumac makes anything taste good.

2 medium cucumbers (about 1½ pounds)

3 tablespoons butter

2 teaspoons sumac (page 101)

Salt and freshly ground black pepper to taste

Thinly slice the cucumbers and layer on paper towels to absorb their moisture.

Heat a large frying pan and melt the butter. Fry the cucumbers over medium-high heat until lightly browned, about 5 minutes, tossing all the time. Add the sumac and salt and pepper to taste. Toss together over the heat for 1 minute more. Serve hot.

Fried Cucumbers
with Leeks

Serves 4 to 6 as a side vegetable dish

I do not suppose that you have ever tried fried cucumbers. They are really quite delicious, although the only culture that I know of that enjoys them in our time is the German.

This is a very tasty dish. Given the fact that cucumbers and leeks were among the few vegetables that were available in Palestine, we can assume that this plate was very much appreciated.

> **2 medium cucumbers (about 1¹/₂ pounds)**
> **4 cups julienned leeks, cleaned and sliced thinly lengthwise**
> **2 tablespoons olive oil**
> **2 tablespoons butter**
> **1 tablespoon chopped fresh parsley**
> **Salt and freshly ground black pepper to taste**

Thinly slice the cucumbers and layer on paper towels to absorb their moisture. Allow to drain for at least 30 minutes.

Trim off the root ends of the leeks and discard. Julienne the white part of the leeks only, discarding the dark green tops. Rinse the leeks in cold water and drain very well.

Heat a large nonstick frying pan and add the oil, butter, and cucumbers. Sauté over medium-high heat for 5 minutes, tossing all the time. Brown the cucumbers and add the leeks and parsley. Sauté for 2 to 3 minutes more, until the leeks collapse. Add salt and pepper to taste.

Desserts on the
Biblical Table

I t is hard for Americans to think of dinner without dessert. (I think we have gone too far in terms of the sugar trip.) Why were desserts not common in Biblical times? It is a simple mystery: They had no processed sugar. Honey and fruit were used as sweeteners, and the sort of thing that we see as dessert could not have existed in the ancient world.

Honey and fruit are not a bad dessert by themselves. In this section we have tried to offer foods of ancient times that still appear in our age, as well as a few sweet things from the early days that I hope you will try.

The only dish in this collection that would have been beyond the grasp of Biblical peoples is the honey cake, a Jewish delight for hundreds of years and a wonder in our time. The rest of these sweets you could probably have found in the streets of ancient Palestine.

Milk and Honey

The Land of Milk and Honey is mentioned in the Bible as an image of hope for a starving people. It is mentioned in each of the first five books of the Bible, the Pentateuch, commonly called the Five Books of Moses, and each claims that the people of Israel, who had been starved for so long, would come to a land of plenteousness, a land that *flowed* with milk and honey. This image must have been incredible for a starving people who had rarely ever seen a river, let alone one flowing with the blessings of milk and honey.

So, one of the great delights for a child in Biblical times was a cup of milk and honey. Make it for your children and talk about the problems of hunger in our time.

Place a pint of milk in a food blender and add two to three tablespoons of honey. (I usually warm my honey in the microwave for a moment so that it will blend well and be frothy. Leave the metal lid off the glass jar, of course.) Whip the mixture for just a moment, then pour it into glasses and serve.

The kids will think it is even better than the sweet milk that remains in the bottom of their cold cereal bowls in the morning.

Honey and Vinegar

This does not sound like dessert to you, does it? In Biblical times this was a special drink offered to guests and, I suppose, on special occasions, to children.

Serve this in very small amounts, of course. Mix a bit of red wine vinegar with a bit of honey and serve. That is it. Just thought you should know!

Sesame and Almond Honey Candy

This is a good guess at what may have been something close to candy in the Old World. All of the ingredients are common, and we have traces of such a dish in contemporary Middle Eastern cultures. So, we developed this recipe thinking that it should work, and it did.

Buy your sesame seeds in bulk at any good Asian grocery. You might buy your almonds there as well. The prices for these items will be much lower than in your local supermarket.

You must have a good candy thermometer for this one.

2 cups honey

1 teaspoon salt

1¹/₂ cups raw sesame seeds

1¹/₂ cups slivered raw almonds

1 tablespoon butter to oil a large plate

Place the honey in a heavy 1-quart saucepan and slowly heat to 212°. Use a candy thermometer to gauge this.

Add the salt, carefully stirring with a wooden spoon so the honey does not bubble over. Stir in the sesame seeds and almonds. Bring the honey to 270°, stirring often. Remove from the heat.

Butter a large kitchen plate or cookie sheet and pour the mixture onto the plate or cookie sheet. Allow to cool.

Cut into small pieces for nibbling.

NOTE: This is a very sticky candy, but I think the kids will love it, especially if you teach them about the history of the dish and they are involved in the preparation.

Honey Cake

Serves 10 to 12

This cannot be traced back to Biblical times, but it has been eaten at Jewish holidays for generations and is a wonderful cake. This recipe is from Fanny Silverstein. She is a very busy Jewish mama who has fed her children well, and her son insisted that she publish a cookbook. She is a Romanian Jewish immigrant and her sense of history in the soup pot is just wonderful. The book is entitled *My Mother's Cookbook,* and this recipe for an overwhelming cake comes from the book.

Mostly Biblical ingredients. OK, the instant coffee doesn't count.

> 3 cups all-purpose flour (see hint on measuring flour, page 178)
>
> 1½ teaspoons baking powder
>
> ½ teaspoon baking soda
>
> ¼ teaspoon ground cinnamon
>
> 1 tablespoon instant coffee
>
> ½ cup boiling water
>
> 1 cup honey
>
> ¼ cup vegetable oil
>
> Grated peel of 1 orange
>
> 2 tablespoons brandy or any whiskey
>
> 4 large eggs
>
> 1 cup sugar
>
> 1 cup chopped walnuts

Combine the flour, baking powder, baking soda, and cinnamon; set aside. Mix the instant coffee with the water; blend in the honey, oil, orange peel, and brandy. In a large bowl, beat the eggs until frothy; gradually add the sugar and beat until light. Add to the honey mixture.

Combine the flour mixture alternately with the honey mixture, starting with flour and ending with flour. Stir in the walnuts.

Pour the batter into an oiled and waxed paper–lined 13- by 9- by 2-inch baking pan. Bake in a preheated 325° oven for about 50 minutes. Test with a toothpick. If moist, continue baking until a toothpick inserted in the center comes out clean.

Invert the cake onto a wire rack. Cool. Peel off the waxed paper and wrap in aluminum foil to maintain freshness.

Yogurt and Honey

Few of us have seen yogurt and honey as an ancient dish. It goes so far back into history that I have not been able to trace it. But it still survives in Greece as a common dessert.

Use our Homemade Yogurt (page 204) and simply drizzle a bit of honey over the dish. This is so refreshing—and talk about up to the minute in terms of the new diet craze. Yes, a diet food from two thousand years ago!

Heaven!

Yogurt and Jam

I am afraid that we think we are very up to date when we put a bit of jam into a plastic carton of yogurt and then charge a fortune for it. Please try making your own yogurt (page 204) and putting it in little cups with a bit of jam. Enjoy it at work during the day and understand that this little dessert goes back to ancient times. Try apricot jam and yogurt, my favorite!

Quince Jam

Makes 4 to 5 pints

This most delicious condiment is a bit of a problem. The problem stems from the nature of the fruit, which, while it goes back to ancient times, is not always dependable in our time. I have purchased quinces from my local produce man in the Pike Place Farmers' Market in Seattle and they were great. But I purchased some at the public market in San Francisco, near the Opera House, and they were nothing but sawdust in terms of flavor. So, I want you to smell the fruit for flavor first of all. It should smell of pear, pineapple, and apple all at once. If it is not ripe yet, then chance a few and let them ripen on the windowsill until you do smell these perfumes. Talk to a produce person you can trust!

This is a very ancient fruit and is mentioned in the Bible many times, though in English translations it is called an apple. Since the apple came from the New World (Johnny Appleseed and all of that), the apple of the Old Testament had to be a quince, not an apple.

It was not an apple that Eve offered to Adam, but rather a quince. Now, that is settled.

This fruit was very popular in the ancient world, and I happen to know that the Queen of Sheba was very fond of the following recipe. Do try it!

Be sure to buy your quinces in the fall and then allow them to sit on the windowsill until they are ripe and fragrant. Then you can use them in cooking.

This is a very versatile jam. We use it for several recipes in this collection.

5 pounds ripe quinces (5 to 7 large ones)

$^1/_2$ lemon

4 cups sugar

Cut the quinces in half from stem to bottom and core them with a paring knife. Rub the flesh of the quinces with the lemon half and set aside. Dice the fruit, with the skin on, and place in a 8-quart pot. (This should yield about 14 cups of cored diced quinces.)

Add just enough cold water to barely cover the fruit (about 6 cups). Bring to a boil, cover, and simmer gently for 5 minutes or until very tender. Drain through a strainer, discarding the liquid. Work the drained fruit through a food mill into the previous pot. Discard any pulp that remains in the food mill. Add the sugar to the milled fruit pulp and simmer gently, uncovered, for about 25 minutes. Stir regularly.

Epilogue

—•—

The quest for the American Dream has brought us to privatism, and with it the destruction of much of what has been very good in terms of our communal life-style in the past. Biblical history intends to bring us back to that communal table, and to a communal understanding of ourselves as a people and as nations of the world.

TV dinners are aimed at privatude. They have no memories such as the great feasts of the past, feasts at which we passed along the meaning of our culture.

How much time do we have left before our culture is no more? Probably until the end of the week, unless we draw together to feast with one another. I mean that!

We finally come, in this discussion, to the feast that is to be the fulfillment of history. II Isaiah 55:1–3 discusses it. In the description, Isaiah quotes the Lord as inviting everyone to come to the table for the feast. And they come, from all of the corners of the earth. And they feast at one table. No enemies present! Tickets for the feast are given out without cost, a strange concept for those Puritan ethicists among us who claim that you don't get something for nothing. Here is the scene:

> Ho, every one who thirsts,
>   come to the waters;
> and he who has no money,
>   come, buy and eat!
> Come, buy wine and milk
>   without money and without
>   price.
> Why do you spend your money for
>   that which is not bread,
>   and your labor for that which
>   does not satisfy?
> Harken diligently to me, and eat
>   what is good,
>   and delight yourselves in fatness.
> Incline your ear, and come to me;
>   hear, that your soul may live;
> and I will make with you an
>   everlasting covenant,
> my steadfast, sure love for David.

It is wonderful to think that everyone you know and love will be present. More important, everyone you cannot stand will be present! All peoples will be gathered at this single table of history. The table will go on for miles, and you will look about and be pleased with everything—well, almost everything. I am convinced that the Holy One will place five persons I cannot stand directly across the table from me, five persons with whom I refuse to deal. Five persons that I will have to see as close friends since there can be no enemies at the table. As a matter of fact, I am so concerned about who those five people will be that I keep a running list of those five. Every time I realize that I must deal with these people, I manage to communicate and heal the wounds with one. My list is down to four! Suddenly, another name appears on my list.

I know your life is the same way, and I am convinced that you have a similar list. The only good this list does us is that it proves we cannot set the table in the presence of our enemies. The Lord has to do that, and will!

The invitation will be open to everyone and the Messiah will pour the wine. Then, we will all lift our glasses to toast one another. I will have to face those five, and you will have to face your five, and I will say to mine, "I don't understand this, but God finds each of you to be totally lovable." Then we will all shout, "L'chayim. To life, because it is of God and because it is good."

And in that moment, at that table, history will at last come home.

I will see you at the feast.

I bid you peace!

Bibliography

Bailey, Adrian. *Cooks' Ingredients*. New York: William Morrow, 1980.

Barash, Cathy Wilkinson. *Edible Flowers*. Golden, Colorado: Fulcrum Publishing, 1993.

Capon, Robert Farrar. *The Supper of the Lamb*. New York: Pocket Books, 1970.

Cullman, Oscar. *Early Christian Worship*. London: SCM Press Ltd., 1953.

Eliot, T. S. *Christianity and Culture*. New York: Harcourt Brace Jovanovich, 1960.

Goodman, Naomi, Robert Marcus, and Susan Woolhandler. *The Good Book Cookbook*. New York: Dodd, Mead, 1986.

Herbert, A. S. *Worship in Ancient Israel.* Richmond, Virginia: John Knox Press, 1959.

Intrepreter's Dictionary of the Bible. Vols. 1–4. New York: Abingdon Press, 1962.

The New Oxford Annotated Bible with the Apocrypha. New York: Oxford University Press.

Richardson, Alan. *A Theological Wordbook of the Bible.* New York: Macmillan, 1960.

Silverstein, Fanny. *My Mother's Cookbook.* New York: Carroll & Graf/Quicksilver Books, 1985.

Tannahill, Reay. *Food in History.* New York: Crown Publishers, 1988.

Thompson, Bard. *Liturgies of the Western Church.* New York: World Publishing Company, 1961.

Von Welanetz, Diana, and Paul Von Welanetz. *The Von Welanetz Guide to Ethnic Ingredients.* Los Angeles: J. P. Tarcher, 1982.

Waldo, Myra. *The International Encyclopedia of Cooking.* Vols. 1–2. New York: Macmillan, 1967.

Wigoder, Devorah Emmet. *The Garden of Eden Cookbook.* New York: Harper & Row, 1988.

Young, Robert. *Analytical Concordance to the Bible.* Peabody, Massachusetts: Hendrickson Publishers, 1984.

Index

fried (*continued*)
  cucumbers with sesame oil and
    coriander, 273
  cucumbers with sumac, 275
  eggs with olive oil and sumac, 171
  lentil cakes, 147
fruit:
  lamb stew with cinnamon and,
    220–221
  salad, biblical, **162–163**
fruit sauce:
  quail simmered in, **250**
  see also individual fruits

Gamaliel, Rabban, 35
game hens:
  fowl stuffed with barley and mustard
    green dressing, **246**
  fowl stuffed with bulgur wheat
    dressing, **244–245**
  fowl with grapes, **244–245**
  with spices, **248–249**
garbanzo beans (chick-peas), 130
  four-grain bread with lentils, **184–186**
  garbanzo-sesame dip (hommus), 107,
    108
  and lentils, **135–136**
  and wheat berries with artichokes,
    138–139
Garden of Eden Cookbook, The (Wigoder),
    153
garlic:
  broiled fish with mint and, **261**
  coarse wheat bread with, **196**
  eggs with yogurt and, **168**
  grilled lamb chops in grape leaves
    with, **225**
  leek fritters with, **272**
  quail with cumin and, **247**
  wheat berries with dill and, **141**
Genesis, Book of, 17–18, 20–21, 40, 47,
    81, 82, 85, 146, 211–212
George Washington's Seasoning and
    Broth, 104
goat fat, applied to armpits, 11
Good Book Cookbook, The (Goodman *et
    al.*), 181, 219, 236
Good Samaritan, Parable of, 53–54
"Grain from Heaven," 9
grains, **127–148**
  baked barley casserole, **133**
  barley casserole with leeks, onions, and
    sesame oil, **145**
  barley with saffron and grapes, **148**
  bulgur wheat pilaf with leeks, **142**
  bulgur wheat pilaf with mulberries,
    143
  Esau's pottage, **146**
  fried lentil cakes, **147**
  lentil and wheat pilaf, **144–145**
  lentils and barley, **137**
  lentils and garbanzo beans, **135–136**
  sprouted, 134–135

sprouted, in pilaf, **144**
toasted barley, **131**
two-grain pilaf with lentils, **132–133**
wheat berries and garbanzo beans with
  artichokes, **138–139**
wheat berries with garlic and dill, **141**
wheat berries with onions and mint,
  140
grape leaves, 107
  buying, 225
  fish wrapped in vine leaves, **262–263**
  grilled lamb chops with garlic in, **225**
  lamb chops grilled with mint and
    cinnamon in, **226–227**
  rolled, with currants and pine nuts,
    112–113
  rolled, with lamb, **111–112**
grapes, 12, 95
  barley with saffron and, **148**
  fowl with, **242–243**
Greeks, 24, 40, 60, 66, 94
grilled lamb chops:
  with garlic in grape leaves, **225**
  with mint and cinnamon in grape
    leaves, **226–227**
  with sumac, **224**

Haggadah, 27, 28
halibut:
  broiled fish with garlic and mint, **261**
  broiled fish with honey and oil, **260**
  fish wrapped in vine leaves, **262–263**
Hebrew language, 4–6, 9, 17, 25, 45,
    47–48
  bread in, 9
  gender in, 86–87
  manna in, 42
  names of God in, 5–6, 9, 23, 86
  oxymorons in, 5–6
  soul in, 24–25, 44–45, 48
Hellenism, 24, 84
  Creation doctrine of, 40
herbs:
  mixed fresh cucumber salad with,
    155
  yogurt cheese with, **207**
  see also specific herbs
Hippolytus, Saint, Eucharist of, 61–66
hommus (garbanzo-sesame dip), 107,
    108
  with dill, **109**
  with sumac and hyssop, **110**
honey, 43, 61, 65, 93, 96
  broiled fish with oil and, **260**
  cake, **282–283**
  candy, almond and sesame, **281**
  milk and, **280**
  and vinegar, **280**
  and yogurt, **283**
Hospitality, Rule of, 16–18, 48
hunger, 6, 9, 11, 16, 24–25, 75, 82, 92
hyssop, 96, 99
  cucumber salad with dill and, 156